THE WHOLE
INTERNAL
UNIVERSE

THE WHOLE
INTERNAL
UNIVERSE

Imitation and the New Defense of
Poetry in British Criticism
1660–1830

JOHN L. MAHONEY

New York
Fordham University Press
1985

THE PUBLICATION OF THIS BOOK WAS MADE POSSIBLE IN PART
BY A GRANT FROM
THE HYDER ROLLINS FUND

FOR
ANN
AS ALWAYS

Poetry holds the outer world in common with the other arts. The heart of man is the province of poetry, and of poetry alone. The painter, the sculptor, and the actor can exhibit no more of human passion and character than that small portion which overflows into the gesture and the face, always an imperfect, often a deceitful, sign of that which is within. The deeper and more complex parts of human nature can be exhibited by means of words alone. Thus the objects of the imitation of poetry are the whole external and the whole internal universe, the face of nature, the vicissitudes of fortune, man as he is in himself, man as he appears in society, all things which really exist, all things of which we can form an image in our minds by combining together parts of things which really exist. The domain of this imperial art is commensurate with the imaginative faculty.

THOMAS BABINGTON MACAULAY,
"Moore's *Life of Lord Byron*"

CONTENTS

Preface   ix

Introduction   1

I Classical Beginnings and Neoclassical Doctrines

1. The Concept of Mimesis: Backgrounds and Development   9

II Restoration and Eighteenth-Century Aesthetics: The Persistence and Widening of an Idea

2. Early Revisions and New Dimensions:
   Dryden, Addison, Burke   21

3. The Anglo-Scottish Critics and Aestheticians:
   Imitation and the New Psychology   49

4. Sir Joshua Reynolds: Freedom and the Tradition   81

III Toward a Romantic Mimesis: The Manifesto-Makers

5. Wordsworth and the Romantic Manifesto   99

6. Shelley: Poetry as the New Religion   112

7. Hazlitt: Imitation and the Quest for
   a Romantic Objectivity   121

IV Formulating a Romantic Aesthetic

8. Coleridge: Romantic Imitation
   and the New Defense of Literature   133

Epilogue   151

Selected Bibliography   155

Index   163

PREFACE

As much as one tries to debunk the familiar ritual of thanks, it simply cannot be avoided. So one takes refuge in "the briefer the better" approach. As in so many of my endeavors, Walter Jackson Bate has played an important role in the evolution of this book. After finishing a short work on Hazlitt's criticism, I came to him with some terribly vague and amorphous ideas about a book on eighteenth-century critical theory. As usual, he insisted that I write down what I wanted to do, and out of some very rough statements came several instructive sessions and the decision to work on the topic of this book. His enormous knowledge and, most important, his bedrock wisdom about literary study and contemporary scholarship are always models of excellence. James Engell listened to my ideas, criticized them, and helped me to find areas for exploration. My colleagues Paul Doherty, Robert Kern, Robin Lydenberg, John McCarthy, Andrew Von Hendy, and William Youngren were always ready to read, to listen, to offer suggestions. None of the above shall take any blame for weaknesses in my work.

I should like to offer special thanks to my graduate research assistants Melinda Ponder and Susan Skees for flawless work. Barbara Lloyd has been a superior typist not afraid to criticize any and all drafts. Patricia Mahoney has once again been a fine adviser on matters concerning design. Dr. Mary Beatrice Schulte of Fordham University Press, that rare combination of cheerful and rigorous editor and scholar, has been the guiding spirit of this book, and she has my deepest gratitude.

I am greatly indebted to the staffs of the Boston College Library, the Wessel Library of Tufts University, the Widener Library of Harvard University, the Beinecke Library of Yale University, and The Yale Center for British Art for many courtesies while I was working at these institutions.

A Mellon Grant that provided released time for research was invaluable for launching this book, and a Boston College sabbatical leave helped me to complete it. Donald J. White, Dean of the Graduate School of Arts and Sciences; Rev. William Neenan, s.j., Dean of the College of Arts and Sciences; Professors Joseph Appleyard, s.j., and Dennis Taylor, my Department chairmen during the period I was working on the book, are the kinds of university administrators who translate con-

ix

cern for scholarship into practical assistance whenever it is needed. Special thanks are also due to The Hyder Rollins Fund for help in the publication of this book.

For support and encouragement throughout this project, I am grateful to Margaret Mahoney, Mary Lou and Neil Hegarty, Dot and Ray Angelone. And, finally, Jackie and Roy Kral—friends and musicians *par excellence*—provided their special kind of inspiration.

INTRODUCTION

I

WHY THE NEED for another study of artistic imitation? There is, to be sure, no dearth of books and articles dealing with the recurring critical concept of poetry—indeed, of art—as mimetic, as imitative of men and women in action. Such studies follow the idea from its origins in Plato and Aristotle to its codification in Roman critics like Horace, to its medieval phase where it takes on sharply religious and didactic overtones, to its neoclassical restatement, sharply conservative in Renaissance theorists like Sir Philip Sidney, and more flexible and open-minded in Restoration and eighteenth-century critics like Dryden, Pope, and Johnson.

Erich Auerbach's massive study *Mimesis: The Representation of Reality in Western Literature*, with its citation and discussion of a variety of literary masterpieces and its description of two major modes of imitation—one more realistic, the other more inward; one more direct, the other more suggestive—is a truly pioneering study.[1] M. H. Abrams' *The Mirror and the Lamp: Romantic Theory and the Critical Tradition*—a sweeping survey of the major statements about literature in the history of criticism—sees an evolution in the posture of critics and theorists from the mimetic emphasis of Plato and Aristotle to the pragmatic or audience-oriented approach of Sidney.[2] With the coming of the early romantic theorists and their emphasis on what he calls the expressive, Abrams views the concern of criticism as moving from external reality to the artist and his expression of personal feeling. A fourth phase, which Abrams calls the objective, emphasizes the work of art as independent object, to be taken up in its own terms and without any special consideration of its connections with the world beyond it, with its audience, or with its author. For Abrams the tradition of imitation has, for all practical purposes, ended by the late-eighteenth century. His book is indispensable for anyone studying shifting concepts of imitation in the period from 1660 to 1830.

1

John Boyd's remarkable book *The Function of Mimesis and Its Decline* is in many ways the stimulus behind the chapters which follow.[3] In a densely historical survey enriched by an illuminating central argument, Boyd sees the mimetic critical tradition as extending, in one form or another, from classical antiquity down to the end of the eighteenth century. It was essentially an objective tradition, "object-oriented, outward-going, especially by comparison with what followed in the nineteenth century and after," although within that tradition there are at least two distinct strains, "one of which sees it as an autonomously meaningful structure, and the other, more rhetorically conceived, which views it as an instrument for molding opinion or moving an audience to action."[4] For Boyd the defense of literature in the mimetic tradition moves from a view of poetry as conveying truth through the very process of representing reality which it employs to a thinner view which regards poetry as a tool for conveying truths external to it. The ancient mimetic tradition, Boyd argues, was eroded as it passed through the conservatism of Roman artistic theory, the religious humanism of medieval and Renaissance criticism, and the scientific rationalism of the Enlightenment. The tradition ended in a great critic like Samuel Johnson, to be replaced by a new subjectivism which carried criticism in drastically new directions. I shall have occasion to utilize and reflect on Boyd's argument as we proceed.

The pioneering work of R. S. Crane on classical criticism and on British criticism from 1650 to 1800 in his celebrated anthology *Critics and Criticism* and in a number of important articles has brought to the fore a variety of issues and problems connected with the idea of art as mimesis and with the sometimes tangled history of that idea.[5] To a lesser extent the work of John Draper on Aristotelian mimesis in eighteenth-century England has considered the problem of how to deal with the classical concept of imitation as it is taken up in a later context, but it is consistently suggestive.[6]

More wide-ranging but no less searching works which discuss the idea of imitation at various points in its history are Jean Hagstrum's *The Sister Arts: The Tradition of Literary Pictorialism and English Poetry from Dryden to Gray*; Walter Hipple's *The Beautiful, the Sublime, and the Picturesque in Eighteenth-Century British Aesthetic Theory*; G. N. Giordano Orsini's *Organic Unity in An-*

cient and Later Poetics: The Philosophical Foundation of Literary Criticism; and Wallace Jackson's *Immediacy: The Development of a Critical Concept from Addison to Coleridge.*[7] There are others, of course, and I shall have the chance to allude to them as we proceed.

II

So much sound work has been done, then, that a new work runs the risk of repetition. This book may not avoid that risk completely. Yet what originally inspired this study was the desire, not to write the kind of book cited above, but to see, as perhaps it has not been seen before in a concentrated way, the idea of imitation as it takes on new shades of meaning from the time of Dryden forward, and to suggest that critics and aestheticians do not so much abandon the idea as struggle to widen its possibilities. Such a widening, they feel, is required in view of the rapid psychological and aesthetic developments of the time—developments which do not so much deny the vitality of external nature as see the equal or even greater vitality of the inner life, the feelings, the imagination—and of the literature which expresses this life. If imitation in its classical roots means the capturing of what is essential in the events and actions of human life, can it not now mean the capturing of what is central in the imaginings and emotions? Can imitation not convey the expression of the inner life with all its nuances? And can such imitation, conveyed in language and imagery of power, not be said to represent the truth of reality?

The answers to such questions are not always positive, but the struggle to deal with them is a continuing one which is always interesting and revealing. More often than not imitation comes to be seen in a broader perspective, suggesting the representation of the whole internal universe and the whole external universe or the interaction between them. Several modern critics provide support for such a view even when they are not specifically concerned with the topic as I am raising it here. M. H. Abrams, always a major figure in the study of the evolution of critical thought, seems to suggest it even though he uses "mimetic" and "expressive" as dramatically different categories. A work of art, he says, describing the expressive

3

but with mimetic shadings, "is essentially the internal made external, resulting from a creative process operating under the impulse of feeling, and embodying the combined product of the poet's perceptions, thoughts, and feelings." As far as the subject matter of the poem is concerned, he includes "the attributes and actions of the poet's own mind" as well as "aspects of the external world," but "these only as they are converted from fact to poetry by the feelings and operations of the poet's mind."[8] Goran Sorban, in a perceptive study of the vocabulary of mimesis, argues: "In so far as 'express' is used as a synonym of the aesthetic sense of mimeisthai (i.e. to represent and manifest something in artistic media by means of likeness) this is within the boundaries of the Greek usage."[9] And M. A. Goldberg, a contemporary critic of romanticism, addresses the issue in commenting on the poetry of Keats. "In speaking of art as representational," he says, "I am not limiting myself to the idea of naturalistic or photographic representation. I recognize that Keatsian poetry—no less than Cubism or Greek tragedy, Surrealism or the sculpture of Michaelangelo, Abstract Expressionism or the comedies of Shakespeare—can be mimetic of the instinctive, the irrational, the imaginative."[10]

Shifting ideas of imitation are also accompanied by a new defense of literature rooted in the notion that literature—indeed, all arts—has its own validity, that the imaginative struggle, when dominated by passion, to represent that passion metaphorically, is a true representation of reality. This new defense of subjectivity, of the authenticity of the individual consciousness, of the powers of metaphor and symbol to convey the complexity of truth, is, furthermore, a turning away from a view of art as speaking picture or adornment of ethical truth, or elegant re-expression of verities commonly held through the ages. It is the harbinger—perhaps not intentionally so—of many contemporary ways of thinking about the work of art as autonomous, with few if any obligations to biography, history, philosophy. It is—again perhaps not intentionally—the stimulus to much contemporary critical theory with its fascination with the text as language, as sign to be encountered by the intelligent, sensitive reader–critic with little if any concern for author, intention, backgrounds.

4

III

This book will not offer a comprehensive catalogue of critical statements about imitation, although such a project is a worthy one. It will rather focus on British criticism from roughly the Restoration to the Romantics. It will also focus on several of a remarkable group of eighteenth-century Anglo-Scottish aesthetician–critics increasingly preoccupied with the psychological dimensions of art and criticism. These critics, although anticipating in many ways the later romantic manifesto, represent no one neat point of view. Some argue that poetry can no longer be regarded as imitative, and must be described with new terms like "descriptive" or "expressive." Others would broaden the scope of the Aristotelian term to include those works of art which represent the widest possible variety of experience.

After an introductory chapter providing background and a context for considering the idea of imitation, there will be chapters on Dryden, Addison, and Burke; on the Anglo-Scottish critics; on Johnson and Reynolds; on Wordsworth; on Shelley; on Hazlitt; on Coleridge. Perhaps the best way to see these chapters is as a series of essays, each one representing an interesting and important episode in the evolution of the term "mimesis" or "imitation" from remote origins in classical thought to full flowering in the theory and practice of the so-called English Romantics.

NOTES

1. Trans. Willard Trask (Garden City, N.Y.: Doubleday, 1957).

2. (New York: Oxford University Press, 1968).

3. (Cambridge: Harvard University Press, 1968; repr. New York: Fordham University Press, 1980).

4. Pp. xi, xii.

5. Abr. ed. (Chicago: The University of Chicago Press, 1952). Richard McKeon's valuable essay "Literary Criticism and the Concept of Imitation in Antiquity" can also be found in the anthology (pp. 147–75), as can Crane's own "English Neoclassical Criticism: An Outline Sketch" (pp. 372–88). See also Crane's "On Writing the History of English Crit-

icism, 1650–1800," *University of Toronto Quarterly*, 22 (1953), 376–91.

Crane's comments on the larger problem of writing a history of this fascinating period in criticism or the more limited one of dealing with one or two issues within that period have been salutary ones for me. I note in particular the following remark from his "On Writing the History of English Criticism, 1650–1800," 382: "When I assert or deny something in criticism, either in setting forth a general position or in discussing writers or works, what I say is conditioned undoubtedly by my taste and sensibility and by my knowledge of the pertinent facts; but I could not say anything at all unless I had in mind a particular problem, or complex of problems, which I wanted to resolve, a set of assumptions or basic distinctions by means of which I could both formulate the problems, as problems of this rather than some other kind, and argue to conclusions about them, and, finally, some notion of the mode of argument best suited to my aims on this occasion."

6. "Aristotelian 'Mimesis' in Eighteenth-Century England," *PMLA*, 36 (1926), 372–400.

7. (Chicago: The University of Chicago Press, 1958); (Carbondale: The University of Southern Illinois Press, 1957); (Carbondale: Southern Illinois University Press, 1975); (Amsterdam: Rodopi, 1973), respectively.

8. *The Mirror and the Lamp*, p. 22.

9. *Mimesis and Art: Studies in the Origin and Early Development of an Aesthetic Vocabulary* (Stockholm: Bonnier, 1966), p. 128.

10. *The Poetics of Romanticism* (Yellow Springs, Ohio: Antioch Press, 1969), p. 8.

I

Classical Beginnings
and
Neoclassical Doctrines

1

The Concept of Mimesis: Backgrounds and Development

> "Now do you suppose that if a person were able to make the original as well as the image, he would seriously devote himself to the image-making branch? Would he allow imitation to be the ruling principle of his life, as if he had nothing higher in him?"
>
> "I should say not."
>
> "The real artist, who knew what he was imitating, would be interested in realities and not in imitations; and would desire to leave as memorials of himself works many and fair; and, instead of being the author of encomiums, he would prefer to be the theme of them."
>
> Plato, *Republic* 599B

> It clearly follows that the poet or "maker" should be the maker of plots rather than of verses; since he is a poet because he imitates, and what he imitates are actions. And even if he chances to take an historical subject, he is none the less a poet; for there is no reason why some events that have actually happened should not conform to the law of the probable and possible, and in virtue of that quality in them he is their poet or maker.
>
> Aristotle, *Poetics* 1451B9

I

THE CONCEPT OF MIMESIS or imitation in art has held a continuing fascination for philosophers, aestheticians, and critics. Its history has been long and complex. Its earliest important appearance was in what may be seen as a Plato–Aristotle dialogue in classical theory, a dialogue in which Plato takes poets to task for the distracting and disturbing effects of their representations.[1] Ultimate reality for

9

Plato, of course, transcends the vale of shadows which men call life and which artists define as the arena of their activity. This transcendent world is one of pure forms unsullied by individual traits or idiosyncrasies, untouched by particularities which rivet the attention on the here and now to the neglect of the persisting and enduring truths. Preoccupation with this world can only blunt the capacity for beholding the other; consequently poets, caught up with representing the persons and events of this world, are disruptive forces in the good society. Stirred by the imaginative flights and emotional struggles of fictional characters in the drama, men are distracted from their proper vocation of beholding the eternal truths and drawn to the lesser business of observing the vagaries of human conflict.

How many observations of Socrates to Glaucon in Book 10 of *The Republic* come to mind! "Speaking in confidence, for I should not like to have my words repeated to the tragedians and the rest of the imitative tribe," says Socrates, "but I do not mind saying to you, that all poetical imitations are ruinous to the understanding of the hearers, and that the knowledge of their true nature is the only antidote to them" (595B). The imitative poet, preferring "the passionate and fitful temper, which is easily imitated," is, for Socrates, like the painter in two ways: "first, inasmuch as his creations have an inferior degree of truth—in this, I say, he is like him; and he is also like him in being concerned with an inferior part of the soul; and therefore we shall be right in refusing to admit him into a well-ordered State, because he awakens and nourishes and strengthens the feelings and impairs the reason" (605A–B). One notes immediately in Socrates' remark a second and powerful objection to the imitative dimension of poetry: its capacity to stir the imaginations and emotions of readers and spectators to such an extent as to shatter the calm rationality that should characterize human beings in their pursuit of truth.

Implicit in these observations is the strong sense that poetry, because of its mimetic bent, cannot in itself convey the truth, that language and metaphor cannot embody what is essential. Poetry gains its value only to the extent that it serves a higher cause, offers an appealing presentation of the world of the forms. Ready to praise Homer as "the educator of Hellas" (606E), he argues that nevertheless "we must remain firm in our conviction that hymns to the gods and praises of famous men are the only poetry which ought to be admitted into our State" (607A). He is especially forceful in his discussion of the emotional power of Greek tragedy and of its popularity among contemporary audiences, not underplaying its artistic strength, but rather pointing to its power to engage an audience totally and to involve it in the psychological plight of the characters. What is always clear is Plato's restricted concept of art, his inability or refusal to see morally educative force in the power of art to stir the feelings and to carry the audience beyond itself into a realization of alternative forms of experience. As Eric Havelock has put it, poetry for Plato "indulges in constant illusionism, confusion and irrationality. This is what *mimesis* ultimately is, a shadow-show of phantoms, like those images seen in the darkness on the wall of the cave."[2]

II

Art has no autonomy for Plato; metaphor can never formulate or express enduring truth. "Hear and judge," Socrates tells Glaucon. "The best of us, as I conceive, when we listen to a passage of Homer, or one of the tragedians, in which he represents some pitiful hero who is drawling out his sorrows in a long oration, or weeping, and smiting his breast—the best of us, you know, delight in giving way to sympathy, and are in raptures at the excellence of the poet who stirs our feelings most" (605C–D). What ultimately results from this seduction of the imagination and emotions is a random sympathy or empathy that turns toward any person or predicament passionately represented. Any sense of discrimination between great and small, general and particular is lost as reason gives way to feeling. Poetry is truly a subversive force unless it draws the mind to the eternal truths, the persisting forms—witness hymns to the gods and praises of heroes. There is indeed little room for poetry in the good society. For John Boyd, two key consequences of the Platonic tradition of criticism—consequences we shall have occasion to examine at several points in this study—are: "first . . . that it never comes to grips with the actual in experience as an essential ingredient of poetry. Secondly, this lack of realism consistently occasions a nonliterary judgment of the function of literature. Poetry tends to become philosophy and ethics, instead of holding its own ground."[3]

III

Aristotle's response—and that seems the proper word—to Plato's views is, to be sure, a celebrated one. Ostensibly writing about the genre of tragedy, he advances and develops in his *Poetics* ideas on the great Greek dramatists—Aeschylus, Sophocles, and Euripides—in such a way that what emerges is an expansive philosophy of art answering many of Plato's objections and yet cutting new ground that not only was to dominate classical thinking, but was to reappear, although with different emphasis, in Renaissance and neoclassical critical thought. Little more than a brief rehearsal of the Plato–Aristotle dialogue and the key emphases of the *Poetics* is required here.

Aristotle meets Plato's objection to poetry squarely on the issue of mimesis, yet with how different an approach, how fresh and vital a concept of mimesis. That concept is to a great extent rooted in his cosmology, his vision of the nature of things. Eschewing any notion of two utterly different worlds, Aristotle sees one world in which the universal and the particular are vital parts, but parts that intersect, interact with, and enrich one another. It is a dynamic paradigm in which forms emerge through concrete particulars and in which concrete particulars gather meaning from their movement toward larger, more general patterns. This is the world which men must know and in which they must discover meaning. The challenge is considerable, and yet Aristotle does not retreat from the fearful ground to treat art as either a photographic reproduction or a faint shadow. He speaks not in highly abstract or technical terminology; he seems more the observer, the investigator, the theorist. He speaks of mimesis as a fundamental human instinct. Using tragedy as his point of reference, he speaks of it as an imitation, a selective process in which the mind confronts the flux of reality and captures the persisting forms. Poetry, he argues, is

> a more philosophical and a higher thing than history: for poetry tends to express the universal, history the particular. By the universal I mean how a person of a certain type will on occasion speak

or act, according to the law of probability or necessity; and it is this universality at which poetry aims in the names she attaches to the personages. The particular is—for example—what Alcibiades did or suffered [1451B5–10].

Art for Aristotle is a more object-centered process, not chiefly concerned with the feelings of the artist or the picture of some better world. "Tragedy, then, is an imitation of an action that is serious, complete, and of a certain magnitude" (1449B24–25). Again, "the objects of imitation are men in action" (1448A1). Plot is the heart of Aristotle's conception, taking precedence over character, thought, diction, spectacle, and melody. Relatively autonomous, it gives structure to the imitation of action. Narrative, like drama, "should have for its subject a single action, whole and complete, with a beginning, a middle, and an end. It will thus resemble a living organism in all its unity, and produce the pleasure proper to it" (1459A18–21). Rather than mirroring the world of ideas or offering some justification or illustration of a moral code, poetry holds meaning within itself. It represents and communicates a living process not requiring reference to an external norm.

Aristotle, it will be remembered, speaks early in the *Poetics* of all the arts imitating not only action but "character" and "emotion" (1447A28)—that is, what S. H. Butcher calls "the characteristic moral qualities, the permanent dispositions of the mind, which reveal a certain condition of the will" and "the more transient emotions, the passing moods of feeling." Although we ought not to read into this emphasis any justification of art as the expression of feeling distinct from its culmination in some form of external action, there is an intriguing suggestion—I shall pursue it further later—of art as imitative not just of actions (the external universe) but also of feelings (the internal universe). It is the breadth of Aristotle's thinking on this matter that catches our attention, and it is this breadth that later critics in the tradition either perceive and develop or fail to come to terms with in their consideration of the imitative aspect of art. Butcher is illuminating in his discussion of this matter. "An act," he says,

> viewed merely as an external process or result, one of a series of outward phenomena, is not the true object of aesthetic imitation. The πρᾶξις that art seeks to reproduce is mainly an inward process,

a psychical energy working outwards; deeds, incidents, events, situations, being included under it so far as these spring from an inward act of will, or elicit some activity of thought or feeling.[4]

Imitation is pleasurable; it is not simply flat duplication. Nor does it have anything to do with following models from the past. A tragedy, by its stirring of the emotions of pity and fear in an organized structure, purges them so that in Keats's phrase "all disagreeables evaporate." As the audience watches the fate of Agamemnon or Oedipus or Medea unfold—characters larger than life yet universal in their significance—the jarring elements of pity and fear are moderated, and we are drawn into a richer awareness of the hero's or heroine's predicament and of its implications for us. It is this awareness felt not only in the mind but in the heart that is important in Aristotle.[5] The play's the thing, to be sure, holding within it the universal and the particular, the larger meaning in the specific action. And yet that meaning is not superimposed, but rather emerges, to be known by the reader or viewer in the totality of his experience. Instead of Plato's insistence on the disruption of the balance of reason and emotion, Aristotle's view has tragedy, and by implication poetry in general, bringing a richer knowledge and insight. Poetry, then, is justified in its own terms—not in terms of philosophy or history or religion.

IV

The concept of art as imitation, so penetratingly examined by Aristotle, continued to have vitality throughout the classical period, especially in Roman critics and rhetoricians like Horace, Cicero, and Quintilian. John Boyd's remarkable study *The Function of Mimesis and Its Decline* not only has examined with great thoroughness and care the Plato–Aristotle dialogue, but has persuasively traced a gradual erosion of the Aristotelian concept of mimesis. That erosion, Boyd argues, can be seen as early as Horace's *Art of Poetry* when the idea of art as independent in its shaping of human experience into graceful forms gives way to the view, still claiming Aristotle as its source, which makes poetry an instrument of instruction, a pleasing mode of expressing the great truths of the ages.[6] That erosion can further be seen in a shift from a vision of art as engaging the full human being—heart and head—through a heightened awareness of truth to a new neoclassical, un-Aristotelian separation of pleasure and knowledge, the pleasure becoming a didactic tool, a sugar-coating of the pill of truth.

The rhetorical–didactic tradition of art as an instrument—at times a highly delightful one—for persuasion, for driving home key concepts of philosophy and religion, for making better citizens, better Christians seemed to dominate the theory and practice of criticism for centuries.[7] Indeed this tradition, firmly established as early as Roman times, was solidified even more, given the religious thrust of art in the Middle Ages. Robert Montgomery has studied the work of five didactic theorists from the Middle Ages to the Renaissance—Dante, Fracastoro, Barbaro, Sidney, and Tasso—to illustrate the vitality of audience-response and didacticism as issues and to point up "the value of fiction primarily in terms of the ends it gains in the mind of the reader and ultimately in his moral behavior."[8] The dividing line between poetry and rhetoric—so clearly defined in Greek and Roman criticism—becomes blurred, with poetry becoming more and more a vehicle for instruction and persuasion, directed more and more toward the will and virtuous action. Speaking of Dante, Montgomery argues:

> There is more than a casual implication that the mind of the spectator and reader must also be initially disposed towards salvation. Given these not inconsiderable conditions, then art can penetrate the imagination and by stages draw the will, the capacity to gaze amorously on good things, to objects we ought to deplore, pity, admire, or covet. By thus engaging the emotions and the mind this divine art teaches us what they are and where they may lead us.

He sees the *Purgatorio* as the perfect didactic poem, tracing, as it does, the movement of the mind toward "the habit of appetite." Here Dante "prepares us for the didactic theory of the Renaissance."[9]

The continuing codification of that theory can be seen in a conservative English Renaissance critic like Sir Philip Sidney and in his major critical statement, *An Apology for Poetry*, published in 1595. Sidney—poet, soldier, scholar, man of the court—reveals, like Ben Jonson and other critics of the time, the influence of sixteenth-century Italian theorists who not only were a part of the Renaissance rediscovery of the *Poetics* but also brought to their work those rhetorical–didactic ingredients just considered. Sidney cites Aristotle as his source as he proceeds to talk about imitation. Poetry, he contends, is the great civilizing force in human history, the speaking picture that combines the best of philosophy and history. The poet combines the "precept" of the philosopher with the "what is" of the historian. "Now doth the peerless poet perform both: for whatsoever the philosopher saith should be done, he giveth a perfect picture of it in some one by whom he presupposeth it was done, so as he coupleth the general notion with the particular example."[10] Poetry is "an art of imitation, for so Aristotle termeth it in his word *mimesis*, that is to say, a representing, counterfeiting, or figuring forth—to speak metaphorically, a speaking picture—with this end, to teach and delight" (p. 101).

While Aristotle seems an obvious Sidney source, Sidney's emphasis is clearly neoclassical, rooted perhaps ultimately in Horace but more immediately in a kind of Christian Platonism or Platonic Christianity. Jean Hagstrum regards this concept of imitation as not Aristotelian at all but rather a Renaissance term "in the more literal sense of late antiquity."[11] How often one hears echoes of Socrates in Sidney's words about imitation: "Nature never set forth the earth in so rich tapestry as divers poets have done; neither with pleasant rivers, fruitful trees, sweet-smelling flowers, nor whatsoever else may make the too much loved earth more lovely. Her world is brazen, the poets only deliver a golden" (p. 100). Where the brazen world offers citizens of every variety, the golden world of the poet offers in Theagenes a speaking picture of the lover, in Pylades a model of the friend, in Orlando a type of the valiant man, in Cyrus an example of the true prince, in Aeneas a portrait of the hero.

Imitation, in a word, captures the transcendent world, and offers models of virtuous action for those beclouded by the moral ambivalence of a shadowy reality. Imitation would serve a higher master, be an instrument of instruction and reformation. It does not discover persisting forms in the flux of process and offer in these forms a deep and pervasive knowledge of essential truth. For Sidney "the skill of the artificer standeth in that *Idea* or fore-conceit of the work, and not in the work itself" (p. 101). "Sidney," argues Forrest Robinson, "conceived of poetry more as an art of presentation than as an established book of knowledge or as a tradition with a definite history. The poet borrows his conceits from the philosopher, transforms them into speaking pictures, and thereby renders teaching delightful." [12]

Sidney's rigid reading and interpretation of Aristotle bespeaks a neoclassical way of thinking about imitation, a way that is limited in range, self-conscious. The objects of imitation are situations and personages external to the artist; they are also ideas, virtues, models that can, by proper pictorial representation, draw the reader or viewer to virtuous action. In the larger context, such a philosophy of art or defense of poetry will not grant autonomy to the poem, for the poem must serve the higher cause of instruction and edification. Poetry has not yet been freed by critics for the representation of the inner life, for the expression of sincere and authentic passion, for the making of images not as audio-visual aids but as self-contained embodiments of the complexities of a rich and mysterious nature. Some first steps are taken in the critical essays of John Dryden, Joseph Addison, and Edmund Burke, and we shall now turn our attention to these.

NOTES

1. For a good survey of Greek and Roman critics, see J. W. H. Atkins, *Literary Criticism in Antiquity*, 2 vols. (Cambridge: Cambridge University Press, 1934). See also McKeon's "Literary Criticism and the Concept of Imitation in Antiquity." Citations from Plato are from *The Dialogues of Plato*, trans. B. Jowett, 2 vols. (New York: Random House, 1937). Citations from Aristotle are from S. H. Butcher, *Aristotle's Theory of Poetry and Fine Arts*, ed. John Gassner, 4th ed. (New York: Dover, 1951).

2. *Preface to Plato* (Cambridge: Harvard University Press, 1963), p. 25.

3. *Function of Mimesis*, p. 18.

4. *Aristotle's Theory*, p. 123. See also Butcher's observation that: "The common original, then, from which all the arts draw is human life,—its mental processes, its spiritual movements, its outward acts issuing

from deeper sources; in a word, all that constitutes the inward and essential activity of the soul" (p. 124).

5. There has, of course, been a continuing debate among critics and translators concerning the precise meaning of purgation and whether that purgation takes place in the action of the play itself or in the audience viewing. See, for example, ibid., pp. 240–73.

6. Pp. 35–50. See also McKeon, "Literary Criticism and the Concept of Imitation," p. 173: "after Plato and Aristotle, who judged literature primarily by reference to its object of imitation, there grew up a generation of critics, of numerous and long-lived progeny, who judged literature by considering its effect on the audience."

7. See J. W. H. Atkins, *English Literary Criticism: The Medieval Phase* (London: Methuen, 1952) and *English Literary Criticism: The Renascence* (London: Methuen, 1947); Walter Jackson Bate, *From Classic to Romantic: Premises of Taste in Eighteenth-Century England* (New York: Harper & Row, 1961); William K. Wimsatt and Cleanth Brooks, *Literary Criticism: A Short History* (New York: Knopf, 1959).

8. *The Reader's Eye: Studies in Didactic Literary Theory from Dante to Tasso* (Berkeley & Los Angeles: University of California Press, 1979), p. 1.

9. P. 92.

10. *An Apology for Poetry, or The Defense of Poesy*, ed. Geoffrey Shepherd (London: Nelson, 1965), p. 107. All references are to this edition.

11. *The Sister Arts*, p. 65.

12. *The Shape of Things Known: Sidney's Apology in Its Philosophical Tradition* (Cambridge: Harvard University Press, 1972), p. 111.

II

Restoration and Eighteenth-Century Aesthetics: The Persistence and Widening of an Idea

2

Early Revisions and New Dimensions: Dryden, Addison, Burke

For the lively imitation of Nature being in the definition of a play, those which best fulfil that law ought to be esteemed superior to the others. 'Tis true, those beauties of the French poesy are such as will raise perfection higher where it is, but are not sufficient to give it where it is not: they are indeed the beauties of a statue, but not of a man, because not animated with the soul of Poesy, which is imitation of humour and passions: and this Lisideius himself, or any other, however biassed to their party, cannot but acknowledge.

JOHN DRYDEN, *An Essay of Dramatic Poesy*

The pleasures of the imagination are not wholly confined to such particular authors as are conversant in material objects, but are often to be met with among the polite masters of morality, criticism, and other speculations abstracted from matter; who, though they do not directly treat of the visible parts of nature, often draw from them their similitudes, metaphors, and allegories. By these allusions a truth in the understanding is as it were reflected by the imagination; we are able to see something like colour and shape in a notion, and to discover a scheme of thoughts traced out upon matter. And here the mind receives a great deal of satisfaction, and has two of its faculties gratified at the same time, while the fancy is busy in copying after the understanding, and transcribing ideas out of the intellectual world into the material.

JOSEPH ADDISON, *The Spectator No. 421*

. . . but still it will be difficult to conceive how words can move the passions which belong to real objects, without representing these objects clearly. This is difficult to us, because we do not sufficiently distinguish, in our observations upon language, between a clear expression, and a strong expression. These are frequently confounded with each other, though they are in reality extremely different. The former regards the understanding; the latter belongs to the passions. The one describes a thing as it is; the other describes it as it is felt.

EDMUND BURKE, *The Sublime and Beautiful*

I

THE POSITION OF JOHN DRYDEN in seventeenth-century English letters is indisputable. A poet, satirist, dramatist, translator, and critic, he embodies many of the ideals of the classical and neoclassical literary traditions. For our purposes his work as a literary critic is most significant. It was T. S. Eliot who declared him "positively the first master of English criticism."[1] Indeed it is the image of Dryden as critical pioneer which quickly captures the imagination of the student. His contributions to contemporary views of nature and art, to the social and comparative dimensions of criticism, to the treatment of the genres—these and others command attention. Although he lived and moved in the great tradition of neoclassicism and knew something of the "burden of the past" and "the anxiety of influence," he is a critic more liberal, more flexible, and more searching than any in the Renaissance and seventeenth century.

It is almost impossible to study Dryden—or for that matter any of his contemporaries—apart from the religious, philosophical, political, and social phenomena of his age. An era marked by incessant warfare between Anglican and Puritan, king and parliament; the ascendancy of Cartesian–Hobbesian rationalism; the dramatic development of natural science; the overturning of the monarchy of Charles I, the civil warfare of 1642–1660, the Restoration, and the Glorious Revolution of 1688, no doubt had an effect on the artist–critic. Perhaps such an age, with its shifting allegiances, doubts, and insecurities, can explain to some extent the so-called inconsistencies in Dryden's career—his shift from Puritan to Anglican to Roman

Catholic in religion, from republican to royalist in politics, from one point of view to another in literary criticism. Perhaps it can help the contemporary reader to understand more fully the rich flexibility that he brings to critical and aesthetic problems.

Even more fundamental to a consideration of the man and his age are the pronounced skeptical tendency of Dryden's mind, brilliantly sketched by Louis Bredvold, and his lifelong zest for literature.[2] These elements account in large part for his critical stance and style, his desire to test rules and doctrines, to be wary of authority for the sake of authority, to be always mindful of current taste—in short, to be flexible and tolerant in the craft of criticism. Hence, against the background of more rigid neoclassic theory, Dryden must be seen as a liberal, defending the tradition, but always searching for ways of broadening it to include whatever is genuinely artistic; insisting on the importance of delight and entertainment; defending the values of form, decorum, and reasonableness, but leaving room for the pleasures of imitation, imagination, and emotion.

II

In order to appreciate Dryden's critical freedom concerning imitation or any one of a number of critical issues, one must measure his statements against the tradition of authority in which he wrote, the tradition of Sidney, Jonson, and Rymer, against the many imposing discussions of the abstract paradigms of epic and drama woven by Hobbes, Davenant, Milton, and others. For Dryden the rules were always important as a heritage of wisdom to be reckoned with, or, as Walter Jackson Bate has suggested, as a means of imitating "an ordered, harmonious nature," as aids to the artist in presenting, "as in nature itself," a well-organized and probable action in which each part "contributes to the central design."[3]

For Dryden, then, art is mimesis or imitation, although it is important to note in his statement a loosening of the classical and neoclassical emphasis on a close rendering of external nature or a capturing of certain moral norms outside the work. Inspiration, he argues, is always the beginning of art. "For my part," he says in *An Essay of Heroic Plays*, "I am of opinion, that neither Homer, Virgil,

Statius, Ariosto, Tasso, nor our English Spencer, could have formed their poems half so beautiful, without those gods and spirits, and those enthusiastic parts of poetry, which compose the most noble parts of all their writings."[4] Inspiration is, however, no occasion for undisciplined self-expression. Nature is a powerful force, to be honored and confronted. It is "still the same in all ages, and can never be contrary to herself," and "the way to please being to imitate Nature, both the poets and the painters in ancient times, and in the best ages, have studied her" (II 134). It is not, however, a mere collection of particulars as disconnected things, but "an idea of perfect nature," and the artist is to set this image "before his mind in all his undertakings, and to draw from thence, as from a storehouse, the beauties which are to enter into his work; thereby correcting Nature from what actually she is in individuals, to what she ought to be, and what she was created" (II 125). Nature is rooted not only in the actions but in the feelings and imaginings of men, and must be imitated accordingly. It is varied and complex, "a thing so almost infinite and boundless, as can never fully be comprehended, but where the images of all things are always present" (I 3). Dryden's great watchwords are: "whatever is, or may be, is not properly unnatural" (I 154).

Given such an image of nature, the artist for Dryden must capture some of the abundance of this nature, its unity and diversity, its joy and sorrow; must—and Chaucer and Shakespeare are his favorite models—give us God's plenty, must see the truth vividly and imaginatively. Art, then, is truly a process of imitation, not duplication. Speaking of the heroic poet in his essay *Of Heroic Plays*, he argues that such a poet "is not tied to a bare representation of what is true, or exceeding probable; but that he may let himself loose to visionary objects, and to the representation of such things as depending not on sense, and therefore not to be comprehended by knowledge, may give him a freer scope for imagination" (I 153).

Dryden, despite his neoclassical orientation, his strong emphasis on common sense, order, and rational control, nevertheless did succeed in freeing imagination from the role as image-making faculty which it had occupied in much seventeenth-century criticism and in arguing the case for its creative potentialities and for the freedom of the artist. Opposing any narrow concept of realism, he clarifies in a vitally new way the concept of mimesis, a way reminiscent more of Aristotle than of the Renaissance codifiers of classical criticism. Praising Homer and Tasso rather than their slavish imitators because they imitated nature and not abstract models of nature, he contends in *Of Heroic Plays*:

> You see how little these great authors did esteem the *point of honour*, so much magnified by the French, and so ridiculously aped by us. They made their heroes men of honour; but so as not to divest them quite of human passions and frailties: they contented themselves to show you, what men of great spirits would certainly do when they were provoked, not what they were obliged to do by the strict rules of moral virtue [I 156–57].

How closely Dryden's line of reasoning anticipates Samuel Johnson's celebrated defense of Shakespeare's kings and senators in the *Preface to Shakespeare*!

Dryden uses a similar argument when considering the merits of rhyme in serious drama. With typical Dryden ratiocination, he meets the charges of those who argue that rhyme violates the principle of imitation in art, that it is not natural, that blank verse, as found in Shakespeare, is more appropriate. Such arguments, he reasons, amount to saying that rhyme is removed from the realism of prose and hence not so natural. Yet, he contends, those who truly understand the nature of poetry and art know that serious plays ought not to offer a mere repetition of conversation, a flat photograph of everyday life.

> If nothing were to be raised above that level, the foundation of Poetry would be destroyed. And if you once admit of a latitude, that thoughts may be exalted, and that images and actions may be raised above the life, and described in measure without rhyme, that leads you insensibly from your own principles to mine: you are already so far onward of your way, that you have forsaken the imitation of ordinary converse [I 148].

To use blank verse is to admit a degree of artistic freedom in imitation; it is only a further step toward the use of rhyme. Tradition, in a narrow, confining sense, has been the villain in the piece. We have, Dryden contends, been intimidated by the delights of Shake-

25

speare and Fletcher and have concluded that "because they excellently described passion without rhyme, therefore rhyme was not capable of describing it. But time has now convinced most men of that error" (I 149). In a word, rigid rules of imitation will not suffice for Dryden.

III

Already in Dryden we can see a further dimension of imitation. There is, however, in discussing such a dimension, a tendency to remove him from his historical and literary context, and such a danger may not be completely avoided here. Yet, granted Dryden's fundamental allegiance to a classical concept of mimesis, there is nevertheless a more wide-ranging concern with art as imitating not just the external world, the actions of men, but also the inner world of thoughts, emotions, imaginings. There is not yet anything so strong as Wordsworth's "spontaneous overflow of powerful feelings" or Shelley's "expression of the imagination" or even the psychological detail of an Addison, an Alexander Gerard, a James Beattie, an Adam Smith. Still there is a decided concern with enriching the idea of nature by including within that idea the whole range of the inner life and by stressing, albeit still in a relatively unsophisticated vocabulary, the power of imagination to imitate that inner life in metaphor. It is early, to be sure, but Dryden has clearly moved beyond Sidney, Ben Jonson, and Hobbes; he must be seen as part of a progressive aesthetics that looks ahead, as part of a drift toward a more subjective criticism, and specifically a more subjective concept of imitation.

We need to listen to Dryden in several contexts. Arguing through his mouthpiece Neander in the *Essay of Dramatic Poesy* against the arguments of the Francophile Lisideius, he contends, " 'Tis true, those beauties of the French poesy are such as will raise perfection higher where it is, but are not sufficient to give it where it is not: they are indeed the beauties of a statue, but not of a man, because not animated with the soul of Poesy, which is imitation of humour and passions" (I 68). Yet Dryden goes beyond even this justification of imitation of the inner life in a work of art, this defense of the poet's power to convey strong emotion in the characters of a drama.

26

In his celebrated *A Parallel of Poetry and Painting*—a later document—he discusses poetry's power to explore the inner feelings of the artist himself. The *Parallel* outlines along classical lines the composition and ordering of the work of art. It then advances the parallel of the title, seeing that the aims of the painter and poet "are the very same; they would both make sure of pleasing, and that in preference to instruction" (II 128). In all this process the Masters can be models not just because they are Masters, but because they are so keenly attuned to nature.

In the latter part of this essay—a part in which Walter Moyle is cited as an important influence—Dryden addresses directly the issue of imitation and the source of pleasure to be derived from the imitative aspect of both poetry and painting. He cites but takes issue with Aristotle's notion that the pleasure of imitation lies in the inquiry into the truth or falsehood of the imitation by the comparison of its likeness or unlikeness with the original. For Dryden the discovery of truth, a true knowledge of nature, gives pleasure, and a lively imitation of it gives even greater pleasure. Poetry and painting "are not only true imitations of Nature, but of the best Nature, of that which is wrought up to a nobler pitch. They present us with images more perfect than the life in any individual; and we have the pleasure to see all the scattered beauties of Nature united by a happy chemistry, without its deformities or faults" (II 137). Poetry and painting at their best do not merely reproduce the "facts" of nature. Governed by rules, to be sure, they are "imitations of the passions, which always move, and therefore consequently please; for without motion there can be no delight, which cannot be considered but as an active passion" (II 137).

IV

Dryden's general approach to criticism, given his general mimetic orientation, is largely in terms of genres or literary types, and of the goals and techniques specifically related to each. He writes often about the drama; witness his *Essay of Dramatic Poesy*, his *Essay of Heroic Plays*, his *Essay on the Dramatic Poesy of the Last Age,* and his specific discussion of tragedy in the *Preface to Troilus and Cressida.* He deals at length with satire in the *Discourse Concerning the*

Original and Progress of Satire, establishing the special function of the genre which is like moral philosophy in its concern with instruction. His approach to the epic poem is seen in works like the Preface to *Annus Mirabilis* and the dedication of his translation of the *Aeneid*.

Dryden is also a force in the development of sociological criticism. Solidly aware of the tradition and its claims, he nevertheless feels that "the genius of every age is different" (I 99) and that the critic must be in touch with the spirit of the age in which a work of art is produced. His treatment of French and English drama is a fine example of comparative criticism, while his remarks on Elizabethan drama, on Chaucer, and on a variety of other topics make him one of the first important eulogistic or appreciative critics. His approach to Shakespeare establishes the dominant method for the best Shakespearean criticism for the next hundred years.

v

Dryden's idea of imitation is refined and enriched as we move from his earliest to his last critical essays. So also is his confidence in the power of a more fully imitative art to move beyond instruction to a broadening of human experience. The most famous of his critical endeavors is *An Essay of Dramatic Poesy* (1668). On June 3, 1665, as four gentlemen sail leisurely down the Thames, a discussion concerning contemporary poetry develops in which two fundamental oppositions emerge—one between the classic and the modern, the other between the Elizabethan and the modern. The first three speakers—Crites, Eugenius, and Lisideius—represent three brands of neoclassicism. Crites is the extremist, arguing that the Ancients had fully discovered and embodied those rules to which the Moderns should conform. Eugenius, unwilling to revere blindly that which is old simply because it is old, favors the Moderns. Lisideius, taking still another approach, praises French neoclassic drama for its exemplification of the classical ideal.

Neander, regarded generally as Dryden's spokesman, and a thoroughly mimetic critic, soon dominates the essay as he recalls Lisideius' earlier definition of a play as a *"just and lively image of human nature"* (1 36), and deplores the fact that too much of the discussion has neglected the implications of the word "lively" in its excessive concern with the word "just." The French dramas, so favored by Lisideius, have regularity, he agrees, but it is often a static, mechanical regularity. They imitate an idea of nature, not nature itself. Shakespeare is for Neander the great exemplar of the best qualities in English drama, a writer who, in spite of his occasional crudeness and irregularity, reveals a "more masculine fancy" and "greater spirit" (1 79). As Robert Hume sees it, imitation was not of a piece in the Restoration, and there are clear signs early in Dryden's career of figurative representation. "According to the theory largely shared by Neander and Lisideius, literature consists of heightened imitation, not so much of actions (which are hard to inflate) as of the passions and humours which constitute human nature."[5]

As I have already noted, one of the most significant features of Dryden's essay is the debate between Crites and Neander over the use of rhyme in serious drama, a debate the implications of which touch the very foundations of Dryden's conception of art and imitation. Crites finds rhyme unnatural, not as proper for the stage as prose or blank verse. Neander, cautious but flexible in approach, contends that blank verse is no more natural than rhyme, that critics have confused the use and abuse of rhyme, and that great art depends on a process of selection and heightening. "A play, as I have said, to be like Nature, is to be set above it; as statues which are placed on high are made greater than the life, that they may descend to the sight in their just proportion" (1 102). The essential truth of art is conveyed by selection and by imaginative intensity. When dominated and triggered by passion, imagination provides a natural representation of that passion.

VI

It is this concern with artistic latitude, with a broader conception of imitation that pervades Dryden's *Defence of an Essay of Dramatic Poesy* (1668), another example of the flexibility of the critic's mind and the wonderful good sense he brings to his examination of literature. Written as an answer to Sir Robert Howard's objection to the defense of rhyme in the original essay, it is a sparkling examination and defense of the foundations of literature. Finding the debate over rhyme a futile one, he argues that it is the aim of art, not to copy nature, but rather to imitate and heighten in order to know its riches better, that "if all the enemies of verse will confess as much, I shall not need to prove that it is natural. I am satisfied if it cause delight; for delight is the chief, if not the only, end of poesy: instruction can be admitted but in the second place, for poesy only instructs as it delights." Distinguishing a freer and more wide-ranging concept of imitation from a narrow and confining one, he stresses the formidable nature of the poet's task: " 'Tis true, that to imitate well is a poet's work; but to affect the soul, and excite the passions, and, above all, to move admiration (which is the delight of serious plays), a bare imitation will not serve" (I 113).

Dryden's desire to free criticism from the rigidly moralistic approach of critics like Thomas Rymer did not exclude a continuing concern for the moral influence of great art, for the truth of poetry. "[M]oral truth," he insists, "is the mistress of the poet as much as of the philosopher; Poesy must resemble natural truth, but it must *be* ethical" (I 121). In opposing Howard's idea that the action of stage plays has no reality, and that plays improbably and flagrantly violate the unities of time and place, he offers a most forceful defense of the truth of imagination and of poetry's imitation of nature. Assigning greater stature to the imagination than the powerfully influential mechanistic psychology of Hobbes did, he sees the faculty as capable of revealing truth through its own special power. "Imagination," he says, "in a man, or reasonable creature, is supposed to participate of Reason, and when that governs, as it does in the belief of fiction, Reason is not destroyed, but misled, or blinded; that can prescribe to the Reason, during the time of the representation, somewhat like a weak belief of what it sees and hears; and Reason suffers itself to be so hoodwinked, that it may better enjoy the pleasures of the fiction." At the same time as imagination, with the consent of reason, creates its representation of the rhythms of life, the mysteries of nature, the relationships of human beings, reason is never "drawn headlong into a persuasion of those things which are most remote from probability" (I 127–28).

VII

Dryden's later career was devoted in large part to modernizing and translating literary classics and to critical writing. In his criticism one senses a continuing gentle conservatism, a certain echoing of the Jonsonian stress on imitation of models, but then there is also a still further broadening of the whole concept of imitation which anticipates a later critic like Sir Joshua Reynolds. His memorable Preface to the *Fables* is mellow and retrospective, a drawing together of the many facets of his approach to literature. It is a striking example of his characteristic effort to mediate between the extremes of much contemporary criticism—between tradition and original genius, between the rule of reason and the rule of imagination, between the moral and aesthetic concerns of art. At the same time it reveals his underlying and consistent allegiance to certain neoclassic ideals which he associated with greatness in literature.

His famous discussion of Chaucer, regarded by Caroline Spurgeon as the first detailed and careful criticism of Chaucer and the first comparison of the English poet with Ovid, reveals most clearly the range of Dryden as a critic—his fundamental dedication to the neoclassic ideal, but also his desire to see the ideal in its full range of possibilities, to leave an appeal open, as Johnson would say, from criticism to nature.[6] Chaucer, like Shakespeare, is, for Dryden, a "rough diamond," a poet with more nature than wit, an unpolished but true genius, a Homer rather than a Virgil. His merits far outweigh his weaknesses. Foremost is his sense of the riches of nature. "Chaucer," he says, "followed Nature everywhere, but was never so bold to go beyond her" (II 258). He possessed a "most wonderful comprehensive nature" (II 262), and assimilated the variety and abundance of the world and the people around him. Concluding his critique of Chaucer with a passage that articulates so movingly his sense of the fullness of the poet's imitative powers, Dryden writes:

> he has taken into the compass of his *Canterbury Tales* the various manners and humours (as we now call them) of the whole English nation, in his age. Not a single character has escaped him. All his pilgrims are severally distinguished from each other; and not only in their inclinations, but in their very physiognomies and per-

sons. . . . The matter and manner of their tales, and of their telling, are so suited to their different educations, humours, and callings, that each of them would be improper in any other mouth. Even the grave and serious characters are distinguished by their several sorts of gravity: their discourses are such as belong to their age, their calling, and their breeding; such as are becoming of them, and of them only. . . . 'Tis sufficient to say according to the proverb, that here is God's plenty [II 262].

VIII

In any discussion of Dryden in the history of the idea of imitation, there is unquestionably a danger of overemphasizing his liberalism, his concern with widening the scope of nature, with providing a broader context for the emotions and imagination in the work of art. He is, after all, still part of an imposing neoclassical orientation which stresses the order of a universe outside the mind and the obligation of art to capture certain enduring truths within that universe. His allegiance to that orientation can be seen in a certain wariness about the predominance of imagination and emotion in a work of art and in a larger commitment to morality in art. Yet Dryden, almost from the beginning of his critical career, consistently strives to see the full ramifications of the classical ideal in a view of art as a stirring imitation of nature, nature seen as both the world around and the world within. Such a view of imitation provides a concurrent view of literature not simply as a tool of philosophy or history, but as a relatively autonomous mode of conveying truth. The distance between the criticism of Dryden and Sidney is considerable. With the growing psychological speculation of the age—a new interest in the workings of the human mind, in the roots of aesthetic pleasure, in the power of words and images—critical theory takes an even more decided step forward, and the idea of imitation receives a more intensive and searching examination. The defense of art continues, but with a new agenda and a new set of critical propositions.

IX

With Joseph Addison British criticism takes a decidedly different direction. Dryden's liberal and flexible leanings notwithstanding,

Addison's psychological orientation, his praise of subjectivity, his analysis of the peculiar pleasures of artistic imitation, his formulation of a more specialized critical vocabulary were strong forces in moving critics to look for new sources of aesthetic pleasure, new ways of talking about the meaning and purpose of art and about its impact on an audience.

On the one hand, Addison is a critic of his time as he writes about Virgil's *Georgics*, about Milton, about Italian opera, about a variety of works of art. He is concerned with elegant expression, with that true wit which embodies in appropriate language the persisting truths of the tradition. For Gerald Chapman, "Addison kept alive one side of the neoclassicism of Dryden, though he wrote with an eye more to society and the good life, in which poetry may be a part, than to a life of good poetry."[7] For our purposes he is part of a growing psychological reaction against the dominant scientific rationalism of his age.

Nothing like complete harmony characterized the intellectual and artistic milieu of the Restoration and early-eighteenth century. There were always those within that framework who, consciously or unconsciously, reacted against the prevailing ideals. What we have in this phenomenon is not by any means a revolt, but rather a gradual undercutting of old tendencies and a similarly gradual buildup of new ones. The roots are many, but certainly a primary one is the empirical psychology of Hobbes and Locke.

Thomas Hobbes, if not the most immediate, was certainly the strongest, force in the growing empiricism of the age, emphasizing the centrality of experience, of sensation, and of reflection as prime sources of knowledge. Poetry is regarded as a vehicle for engaging the minds of others and for moving those minds to action. In a strongly mechanistic and at times confusing description of the creative process, he associates wit and fancy with invention or quickness in imagining, disposition with judgment, and elocution or expression with the proper adornment of thought or idea.[8] For our purposes what emerges is basically a wit–judgment distinction fundamental to the criticism of the period, with one the power of combination and association (Chaucer and Shakespeare are cited as prime examples) and the other the power of discerning and differentiation (Davenant and Ben Jonson are cited as models). In the midst of this larger framework what stands out is the emphasis on wit, or really imagination at least in a limited sense, on the power of mind to combine sensations into something like a new reality. We are still a long way from romantic ideas of imagination, but strong roots have been set down by Hobbes.

If Hobbes is a beginning point in British empirical psychology, John Locke is the dominant exponent, the developer and refiner, of many Hobbesian ideas. His influence in the eighteenth century was enormous. Every student, regardless of field of specialization, was advised to study his *Essay Concerning Human Understanding* during the second year at any English university. Thomas Gray attempted to versify the entire work in a Latin poem in 1740. Warburton's sweeping statement in a letter to Richard Hurd that " 'Locke is universal' " is an elaborate tribute to the power of his ideas.[9] Locke's key ideas are embodied in the *Essay Concerning Human Understanding* published in 1690. His central thesis is that all human knowledge is derived from sensation or from reflection upon sensation, when the mind turns its view inward upon itself, and observes its own actions about those ideas it has received from without. Matter possesses certain primary qualities like bulk or shape; these qualities are really in things. Secondary qualities— color, smell, sound—do not inhere in things, but come from the mind of men. In a word, Locke offers an image of the mind as active, as bringing to nature more than is actually there. Locke further advances the powerful notion of the association of ideas, the notion that sequences of ideas pass through our minds determined not so much by logic as by certain emotional suggestions.[10]

The implications of the philosophy of Hobbes and Locke were enormous. Ostensibly rationalists, they nevertheless gave impetus to the power of mind, to the ability of imagination to shape and color external reality. For literary theory and criticism the implications were especially strong. W. J. Bate speaks of criticism "follow[ing] the lead of formal empirical psychology" and turning inward "upon the mind itself, hoping, through psychological analysis, to discover at least some common principles of human feeling and human reaction by which some standard of taste could be roughly determined."[11] Emerson Marks contends that what "finally permitted a sounder idea of artistic imitation was the new psychology which was gradually developed from the empiricism of Locke." He sees the most important result for criticism "in turning attention from the work to the mind of the reader or audience, which in turn led to an increasingly articulate distinction between the imaginative and rational faculties." Critics began to see the limitations of the older mimesis and the distortion of reality it offered. They also gave up the attempt to formulate "a complete definition of imitation and turned instead to inquire 'what it is for the imagination to be delighted with,' as Sir Joshua Reynolds phrased it. . . ."[12]

X

Addison's *Spectator* papers "On the Pleasures of the Imagination" are clearly touched by the Lockean spirit; they everywhere reveal psychological inquiry at work. Addison seems vitally interested in just how the mind works, how the artist creates, but also in the peculiar pleasure and truth conveyed by art. His answers to these questions are consistently rooted, not in some fixed external norm of nature, but in the peculiar subjective response triggered by nature and acted upon by the imagination. William Youngren, one of several critics who see in Addison's work the beginnings of eighteenth-century aesthetics, views such an approach as unusual, given the age. An older way of looking at the mind has given way to an eighteenth-century "concern with the mind's temporal operation, in the experiencing of literature and other language, that was eventually to produce the elaborate associationist theories of Alison, Knight, Stewart, and others."[13]

Imitation is at the heart of Addison's aesthetic, with the focus on the inward.[14] There is, of course, still room for a more Aristotelian–neoclassical approach concerned with the representation of persons and things external to the human mind. We are, in fact, pleased by seeing "what is great, uncommon, or beautiful" (No. 409, p. 178). Sight is "the most perfect and most delightful of all our senses. It fills the mind with the largest variety of ideas, converses with its objects at the greatest distance, and continues the longest in action without being tired or satiated with its proper enjoyments" (No. 411, p. 175). Sight cannot be satisfied by the abstract or the artificial,

35

by nature seen in small units. Only "the largeness of a whole view, considered as one entire piece," can accomplish the task (No. 412, p. 178).

Thus far Addison is speaking only of the primary pleasures of imagination, those which arise from actually looking at and contemplating objects outside the mind. As satisfying as these are, they are relatively primitive compared to the more subtle delights of the secondary pleasures. Here the concept of imitation is much more subjective; what is involved is a collaboration of nature and imagination, each one giving to and receiving from the other. God has indeed surrounded us with a glorious creation filled with natural beauties, capable of stirring pleasing ideas in the imagination.

The secondary pleasures of the imagination come, not from any kind of photographic imitation, but from suggestive imitation. We are delighted most of all, he argues, by the kind of representation that provokes us to compare an original with the representation. What is involved is a pleasurable activity of mind:

> Things would make but a poor appearance to the eye, if we saw them only in their proper figures and motions: and what reason can we assign for their exciting in us many of those ideas which are different from anything that exists in the objects themselves, (for such are lights and colours) were it not to add supernumerary ornaments to the universe, and make it more agreeable to the imagination? We are everywhere entertained with pleasing shows and apparitions, we discover imaginary glories in the heavens, and in the earth, and see some of this visionary beauty poured out upon the whole Creation; but what a rough unsightly sketch of Nature should we be entertained with, did all her colouring disappear, and the several distinctions of light and shade vanish [No. 413, p. 182]?

Lest there be any confusion concerning the source of these ideas on the pleasures of the imagination, Addison directs the reader to their source in Locke's *Essay Concerning Human Understanding*, assuming that this reader is generally familiar "with that great modern discovery, which is at present universally acknowledged by all the enquirers into natural philosophy; namely, that light and colours, as apprehended by the imagination, are only ideas in the mind, and not qualities that have any existence in matter" (No. 413, p. 183).

XI

These ideas on the secondary imagination suggest a whole theory of artistic imitation, indeed a whole theory and defense of art. What is involved at root is no wildly romantic idea of creation as pure self-expression, of creation solely out of the energies of the individual mind, but rather an interaction of mind and nature, with mind highlighting specific aspects of nature, heightening nature in such a way that the audience sees it more fully, more brilliantly. Imagination, in the words of one critic, becomes a means of grace.[15] Such a power must be cultivated fully; the poet must form his imagination just as surely as the philosopher must nourish his understanding.

How precisely does the imagination work in the process of imitation? At one extreme is the flight of fancy, Dryden's "fairy way of writing" in which the artist creates out of his own invention a world of spirits. More subtly the poet, through the medium of a fertile and suggestive language and imagery, conveys a deeper sense of the riches of nature as felt by him. He would indeed stimulate the imaginations of readers and viewers to fill out a barer view of nature.[16] As a result, and we note the shift of focus to the imaginative activity of the audience, "this secondary pleasure of the imagination proceeds from that action of the mind, which compares the ideas arising from the original objects, with the ideas we receive from the state, picture, description, or sound that represents them" (No. 416, p. 191). In a section of *Spectator No. 416* which seems to proceed from the classical concept of art as a worthy rival of nature and yet which seems to go beyond it in providing an explanation, Addison explains the roots of imitation and the pleasures it provides. Words, he says, often provide a more lively sense of a scene than the view of the actual scene. The artist, with his vigorous touch, his lively powers of description, "seems to get the better of Nature." In effect, the non-literal representation is more powerful, more true to the way things really are in their variety, complexity, mystery. There is in Addison no suggestion that such imitation is

37

distortion, is fanciful description. Quite the contrary, it is a selective process that heightens, indeed exaggerates, what is essential in nature in such a way, as Keats would say, that "all disagreeables evaporate."[17] The poetic view is more expansive, more penetrating, more stirring.

XII

It is important to linger on this point since often there is a tendency, while exploring the subjective drift of aesthetics in Addison and for that matter in the age generally, to suggest that the new emphasis is on the non-representational, on art as escapist, on the artist as self-indulgent creator of his own world, a world increasingly remote from reality. Although there is no denying the subjective emphases of Addison's ideas on imitation and imagination, at the same time he never, in turning the focus of criticism inward, loses sight of art's fundamental mission to capture the persisting truths of nature. Furthermore, by provoking all the resources of the inner life—mind, imagination, feelings—art provides a more intensive and comprehensive sense of the many facets of experience, of the whole internal as well as external universe. It also satisfies the yearning in men for the perfection in nature, for a sense of order and form which the mere objects and events of nature do not offer. In a striking passage Addison celebrates the triumph of imagination, which "can fancy to itself things more great, strange, or beautiful, than the eye ever saw, and is still sensible of some defect in what it has seen; on this account it is the part of a poet to humour the imagination in its own notions, by mending and perfecting nature where he describes a reality, and by adding greater beauties than are put together in nature, where he describes a fiction" (No. 418, pp. 198–99).

In Addison's papers on the pleasures of the imagination, we see old and new, traditional and innovative. Anchored in the classical and neoclassical view of art as meaningful representation of experience articulated in graceful forms for the pleasurable instruction of an audience, Addison is an early example of the probing aesthetician, someone who, as Gerald Chapman puts it, "did more to loosen up neoclassicism, and ultimately to undermine it, than any other critic in the first half of the century." [18] His criticism offers a richer view of nature and human experience, a more nuanced theory of the imitative process, a pioneering defense of the imagination's power to shape reality and of art's magical gift of enabling its audience to grasp the fullness of that reality intellectually and emotionally.

XIII

Edmund Burke does not immediately evoke the image of the aesthetician or literary critic. Our sharpest memories are perhaps of Burke the statesman, member of Parliament for twenty-nine years, Secretary of the Rockingham Whig Party, forceful spokesman for the rights of the oppressed Irish, for conciliation with the American colonies and against the ravages of the French Revolution and the corruptions of the East India Company. Yet early in his career he wrote a major document—*A Philosophical Enquiry into the Origin of Our Ideas of the Sublime and Beautiful*—a document whose ideas on beauty, sublimity, imagination, and a host of other topics cut new ground not only in his own age, but also in the larger context of aesthetics and critical thought.

Born in Dublin in 1729, he had his early education at the school of Abraham Shackleton the Quaker. His higher education was at Trinity College, Dublin, where he first showed an interest in the law but, having been sent to London to pursue formal legal studies, he found them sterile and unsatisfying and ultimately abandoned them. At Trinity College he also developed a strong interest in psychology, in human motivation, and in the sources of aesthetic pleasure. It was here in 1747 that as a "youth of varied experience, retentive memory, and an acute observer of men and manners . . . he drafted the work which appeared ten years later as the *Sublime and Beautiful*." [19] The treatise was published on April 21, 1757, and it was his only work on aesthetics during a long and active career.

XIV

Burke was, of course, not the first to advance ideas on the sublime and beautiful during the late-seventeenth and the eighteenth centuries. Boileau's translation of Longinus' *On the Sublime* in 1674 had stirred widespread interest. We have already noted the important work of Addison in *The Spectator* papers on "The Pleasures of the Imagination," in which he describes the special pleasures conveyed by "the prospects of an open champaign country, a vast uncultivated desert, of huge heaps of mountains, high rocks and precipices, or a wide expanse of waters, where we are not struck with the novelty or beauty of the sight, but with that rude kind of magnificence which appears in many of these stupendous works of nature." Such pleasures are not calm or completely rational. "We are flung into a pleasing astonishment at such unbounded views, and feel a delightful stillness and amazement in the soul at the apprehension of them" (No. 412, p. 178). But Addison, although a major force in eighteenth-century aesthetics and a pioneer in advancing the claims of the sensuous in literary criticism, made few of the elaborate and radical distinctions between beauty and sublimity and of the detailed analyses of the causes of sublimity which were to attract so many readers to Burke.[20] John Dennis in *The Grounds of Criticism in Poetry* stressed the passionate dimension of the sublime, but with a strongly religious orientation not present in Burke's treatise. Other critics, and a good many poets of the age, explored the sublime if not always in a technical, well-defined manner.

Longinus' first-century treatise *On the Sublime* is, of course, a starting point for any examination of the idea of the sublime. It is a seminal document in the classical tradition of criticism, although it advances several major emphases that are notably at odds with, for example, the positions of Aristotle or Horace. On the one hand, there is the classical emphasis: "In general, consider those examples of sublimity to be fine and genuine which please all and always. For when men of different pursuits, lives, ambitions, ages, languages, hold identical views on one and the same subject, then that verdict which results, so to speak, from a concert of discordant elements makes our faith in the object of admiration strong and unassailable." On the other, there is the new, somewhat romantic emphasis on the superiority of original genius to tradition, on the transcendent, on the superiority of strong emotion to reason in art and criticism. What is most important in Longinus, and here he is different from his eighteenth-century followers, is style, a vigorous language, a grandeur of imagery, and intensity of expression that conveys a great thought powerfully. "The effect of elevated language upon an audience is not persuasion but transport. At every time and in every way imposing speech, with the spell it throws over us, prevails over that which aims at persuasion and gratification. Our persuasions we can usually control, but the influences of the sublime bring power and irresistible might to bear, and reign supreme over every bearer."[21] The rhetorical thrust of Longinus is clear as he emphasizes a certain externality, a set of great thoughts rendered sublime by the force of language. There is not the strong contention, as in Burke, that sublimity is a state of soul occasioned by certain aspects of nature, that it is a psychological state that can be triggered by the power of the artist.

XV

Burke's is a new and distinctive approach to analyzing and discussing the sublime, complete with terminology, psychological apparatus, and a full-blown distinction between beauty and sublimity. He offers a closer examination of the process of imitation and formulates an emerging distinction between the method of poetry and that of other arts like painting. Words like "sympathy" and "description" become part of a vocabulary that attempts to define the process more accurately.

Poetry for Burke is not strictly an imitative art in the way painting is. Poetry and rhetoric seek "to affect rather by sympathy than imitation; to display rather the effect of things on the mind of the speaker, or of others, than to present a clear idea of the things themselves. This is their most extensive province, and that in which they succeed the best" (p. 172). It is, however, imitative in the sense that it describes the rhythms of the inner life—for Burke a less exact kind of imitation in that language does not resemble the ideas and feelings it struggles to express. But poetry does capture the state of the spirit. "It is," he says, "indeed an imitation so far as it describes the manners and passions of men which their words can express; where *animi motus effert interprete lingua*. There it is strictly imitation; and all merely *dramatic* poetry is of this sort. But *descriptive* poetry operates chiefly by *substitution*; by the means of sounds, which by custom have the effect of realities" (p. 173). Words, of course, are problems, both possessing and lacking power and challenging us to distinguish between clarity and force in expression. Too often clarity and force are confused, and consequently poor critical judgments are made. Actually, where a clear expression concerns the reason or understanding, a strong one concerns the passions. "The one describes a thing as it is; the other describes it as it is felt" (p. 175).

XVI

It is this area of the validity of things felt that Burke is most concerned with in his discussion of imitation and the larger issue of the sublime. For him the inner life is authentic and needs to be represented. Poetry is one of the most noble forms of representation, although its medium is not always clear. As more than one critic has observed, he is an uncompromising sensationalist, one who separates perception from judgment. "The imagination," James Boulton argues, "works by regrouping images received from the senses; it is pleased or displeased 'from the same principle on which the sense is pleased or displeased with the realities'. . . . It is by the imagination, too, that the passions are aroused: these again do not operate 'in an arbitrary or casual manner, but upon certain, natural and uniform principles'."[22]

In distinguishing the sublime and beautiful, Burke further clarifies his idea of the imitative dimension of art.[23] Beauty is form and order; it is something external; it appeals to the reason and produces a calm in the beholder. Sublimity is a subjective state, a state of mind occasioned by an appropriate subject. The sublime artist is primarily concerned not with reproduction but with imitation in the fullest sense. "The proper manner of conveying the *affections* of the mind from one to another, is by words; there is a great insufficiency in all other methods of communication; and so far is a clearness of imagery from being absolutely necessary to an influence upon the passions, that they may be considerably operated upon without presenting any image at all, by certain sounds adapted to that purpose . . ." (p. 60).

42

Burke deals at great length with examples of the sublime, and his break with the idea of object formulas or signs is a key point to observe. His chief interest is not in the object as such, but rather in the power of the object, on the one hand, to embody a state of soul and, on the other, to affect an audience strongly. The idea of mimesis or imitation is not so much challenged as widened to include a whole range of psychological responses. "Burke," says Martin Kallich, "uses the new Humean principles of association to implement his refutation of the theory of imitation and the *ut pictura poesis* precept. In accordance with these associationist principles, he finds it possible to argue against exact imitations and descriptions and shaping of a work of art." That principle, and here Kallich suggests not so much an anti-mimetic as an anti–narrowly-mimetic approach, is the one set forth by Edward Young in his celebrated *Conjectures on Original Composition*: "the romantic notion of approximating the spirit of things rather than of copying accurately and perhaps coldly."[24]

XVII

We sense, in reading Burke's essay, that the young aesthetician is struggling mightily with the problem of the inner life, of human motivation, of a view of nature and art comprehensive enough to include the external and the internal universe. The "sublime," he writes as he attempts to frame a critical vocabulary, produces "astonishment," "that state of the soul, in which all its motions are suspended, with some degree of horror" (p. 57).

Obscurity, power, vastness, infinity—these are among the chief sources of the sublime, taking hold of the total human person in a way that compels attention and passionate involvement. Burke can quickly move from aesthetic and critical premises to discussion and analysis of particular literary figures—The Book of Job, Virgil, Spenser, Milton, others. The great writers for Burke exemplify those inner powers of imagination and emotion, and their works reveal the ability of language both to express and to arouse passion.

Edmund Burke, along with Dryden and Addison, represents an interesting and important tradition in British criticism and aesthetics. Keenly in tune with the classical and neoclassical view of art as imitation of nature, they nevertheless would explore the idea of nature more fully. Increasingly systematic as we move from Dryden to Addison to Burke, criticism takes on more and more psychological dimensions. Dryden, the sensitive poet and critic, argues for the imitation of passion as part of poetry's larger responsibility. Addison, as arbiter of neoclassic taste, would look beyond the more obvious pleasures of imagination to those that art can provide through a stirring of the mind by representations that are both vague and stimulating. Burke, perhaps the most thoroughgoingly psychological, offers a full-blown theory of sublimity in art which brings to the fore aspects of nature hitherto deemed unsuitable and which makes the reader not just a spectator but a participant in nature's wondrous process.

Clearly, to suggest that Dryden, Addison, and Burke stand alone in a growing drift toward subjectivity is to ignore the many critics who deal with the imagination and emotions in the age. These three, covering a period of a century or better, represent major figures who regard imitation as more than copy, knowledge as more than a purely intellectual matter, art as more than adorned philosophy. Dryden in a sense demands the questions that Addison addresses, and Burke offers detailed analyses of these answers. And, as James Boulton argues, "More, then, than those of his contemporaries, Burke's theory looks forward tentatively to Wordsworth and Coleridge with their insistence that language, and poetic imagery, must be modified by intense and relevant emotion before poetry can be great."[25] More and more critical theory in Britain focuses on the inner life, on principles of taste rooted in the way human beings really are, on the justification of poetry as the profoundly mimetic rendering of the many sides of reality.

NOTES

1. *John Dryden: The Poet, the Dramatist, the Critic* (New York: Holliday, 1932), p. 51.

2. *The Intellectual Milieu of John Dryden* (Ann Arbor: University of Michigan Press, 1934).

3. *Criticism: The Major Texts* (New York: Harcourt, Brace, 1952; repr. New York: Harcourt, Brace, Jovanovich, 1970), p. 126.

4. *Essays of John Dryden,* ed. W. P. Ker, 2 vols. (New York: Russell & Russell, 1961), I 152–53. All citations from Dryden are from this edition.

5. *Dryden's Criticism* (Ithaca: Cornell University Press, 1970), p. 204.

6. *Five Hundred Years of Chaucer Criticism and Allusion, 1357–1900,* 3 vols. (New York: Cambridge University Press, 1925; repr. New York: Russell & Russell, 1960), I xxxvii.

7. *Literary Criticism in England, 1660–1800* (New York: Knopf, 1966), p. 235.

8. See chap. 8 of the *Leviathan,* in *The English Works of Thomas Hobbes of Malmesbury,* ed. Sir William Molesworth, 11 vols. (London: Bohn, 1839–1845), III 57: "And whereas in this succession of men's thoughts, there is nothing to observe in the things they think on, but either in what they be *like one another,* or in what they be *unlike,* or *what they serve for,* or *how they serve to such a purpose*; those that observe their similitudes, in case they be such as are but rarely observed by others, are said to have a good wit; by which in this occasion, is meant a *good fancy.* But they that observe their differences, and dissimilitudes; which is called *distinguishing,* and *discerning,* and *judging* between thing and thing; in case, such discerning be not easy, are said to have a *good judgment."*

See also chap. 10, sect. 3, of the *Treatise of Human Nature,* in ibid., IV 56: "For, to judge is nothing else, but to distinguish or discern: and both *fancy* and *judgment* are commonly comprehended under the name of *wit,* which seemeth to be tenuity and agility of spirit, contrary to that restiness of spirits supposed in those that are dull."

9. See Kenneth MacLean, *John Locke and English Literature of the Eighteenth Century* (New Haven: Yale University Press, 1936; repr. New York: Russell & Russell, 1962), pp. 1–2.

10. See the crucial passage in John Locke, *An Essay Concerning Human Understanding,* ed. Peter H. Nidditch (Oxford: Clarendon, 1975), p. 104: "Let us then suppose the Mind to be, as we say, white Paper, void of all characters, without any *Ideas*; How comes it to be furnished? Whence comes it by that vast store, which the busy and boundless Fancy of Man has painted on it, with an almost endless variety? Whence has it all the materials of Reason and Knowledge? To this I answer, in one word, From *Experience*: In that, all our Knowledge is founded; and from that it ultimately derives it self. Our Observation employ'd either about *external, sensible Objects; or about the internal Operations of our minds, perceived and reflected on by our selves, is that, which supplies our Understandings with all the materials of thinking.* These

two are the Fountains of Knowledge, from whence all the *Ideas* we have, or can naturally have, do spring."

See also pp. 134–35 for Locke's notion of the primary and secondary qualities of matter.

11. *Criticism: The Major Texts*, p. 271.

12. *The Poetics of Reason: English Neoclassical Criticism* (New York: Random House, 1968), pp. 38–39. See also in this connection Martin Kallich's comprehensive study *The Association of Ideas and Critical Theory in Eighteenth-Century England: A History of a Psychological Method in English Criticism* (The Hague & Paris: Mouton, 1970). Observations like the following (pp. 15–16) point up the strong influence of British empiricism and of its theory of association: "From Hobbes and Locke to Alison and Wordsworth, there were thinkers and critics who believed that principles of art must be founded on principles of human nature, or, to be more precise, that critical doctrines and standards of taste must be interpreted according to the accepted mental science of the period—the operations of the mind known as the association of ideas. The meaning of this term is here outlined at the expense of details. These details are now in order: they are conclusive proof of the extent to which the theory of association, beginning with Hobbes and Locke, affected the literary mind and permeated theories of criticism and taste in England during the eighteenth century."

13. "Addison and the Birth of Eighteenth-Century Aesthetics," *Modern Philology*, 79, No. 3 (February 1982), 283.

14. Citations from Addison are from *Critical Essays from The Spectator by Joseph Addison, With Four Essays by Richard Steele*, ed. Donald F. Bond (Oxford: Clarendon, 1970). The number of *The Spectator* followed by the page number in Bond's edition is in parentheses after quotations.

15. Ernest Tuveson, *The Imagination as a Means of Grace: Locke and the Aesthetics of Romanticism* (Berkeley & Los Angeles: University of California Press, 1960).

16. James Engell's remarks on the secondary imagination, especially those in which he connects the imagination with the imitative dimension of art, are instructive. The secondary imagination, he says, "gives rise to art as an imitation (not a copy) and supplement to nature. Mimesis, the classical foundation of art, becomes an imaginative act. We create by imagination and also appreciate through it, for the pleasure of art derives from that comparison with nature which the art work forces us to make." See *The Creative Imagination: Enlightenment to Romanticism* (Cambridge: Harvard University Press, 1981), p. 37.

17. Wallace Jackson in *The Probable and the Marvelous: Blake, Wordsworth, and the Eighteenth-Century Critical Tradition* (Athens: University of Georgia Press, 1978) writes perceptively on the problem of imitation and feigning in Addison's aesthetic. "Addison," he says, "avoids any implication that art is a feigning or falsehood. On the contrary, art conveys its own truth, one that is more lively, affecting the mind far more vigorously than do similar impressions derived from nature" (p. 22). See also Jackson's discussion of what he calls a "new doctrine"—originating in the mid-eighteenth century—"which emphasized not the mimetic–reflective powers of the artist, but rather that special quality possessed by the highest genius for taking us directly into the ambience of his invention and causing us to experience it immediately" (p. 6). Jackson's study of this doctrine in his *Immediacy: The Development of a Critical Concept from Addison to Coleridge* (Amsterdam: Rodopi, 1973) has been most helpful in the course of my study.

18. *Literary Criticism in England, 1660–1800*, p. 236.

19. Edmund Burke, *A Philosophical Enquiry into the Origin of Our Ideas of the Sublime and Beautiful*, ed. J. T. Boulton (London: Routledge & Kegan Paul; New York: Columbia University Press, 1958), p. xvii. All citations from the essay are from this edition.

20. See, for example, in Engell's *Creative Imagination*, p. 148: "Burke in general follows the lead of Addison that it is the imagination, with its ability to arouse passions and feelings and with its openness to the suggestions of words, that naturally forms the basis of all imitations. But then Burke calls attention to the 'affecting arts', those that engage us completely in their subject. This form of imitation relies on sympathy, which thus appears as a certain kind of imagination—imagination capturing the full nature of a thing or person in all its emotional and associational involvements."

21. Longinus, *On the Sublime*, ed. W. Rhys Roberts (Cambridge: Cambridge University Press, 1907), pp. 57, 43.

22. Burke, *Philosophical Enquiry*, p. xxxv.

23. Burke's strongest statement of the distinction is perhaps the one found in Part 3, sect. 27: "For sublime objects are vast in their dimensions, beautiful ones comparatively small; beauty should be smooth, and polished; the great, rugged and negligent; beauty should shun the right line, yet deviate from it insensibly; the great in many cases loves the right line, and when it deviates, it often makes a strong deviation; beauty should not be obscure; the great ought to be dark and gloomy; beauty should be light and delicate; the great ought to be solid, and

even massive. They are indeed ideas of a very different nature, one being founded on pain, the other on pleasure; and however they may vary afterwards from the direct nature of their causes, yet these causes keep up an eternal distinction between them, a distinction never to be forgotten by any whose business it is to affect the passions" (p. 124).

24. *Association of Ideas and Critical Theory in Eighteenth-Century England*, pp. 148–49.

25. Burke, *Philosophical Enquiry*, p. lxxviii.

3

The Anglo-Scottish Critics and Aestheticians: Imitation and the New Psychology

If the poet, after all the liberties he is allowed to take with the truth, can produce nothing more exquisite than is commonly to be met with in history, his reader will be disappointed and dissatisfied. Poetical representations must therefore be framed after a pattern of the highest probable perfection that the genius of the work will admit:—external nature must in them be more picturesque than in reality; action more animated; sentiments more expressive of the feelings and character, and more suitable to the circumstances of the speaker; personages better accomplished in those qualities that raise admiration, pity, terror, and other ardent emotions; and events, more compact, more clearly connected with causes and consequences, and unfolded in an order more flattering to the fancy, and more interesting to the passions. But where, it may be said, is this pattern of perfection to be found? Not in real nature; otherwise history, which delineates real nature, would also delineate this pattern of perfection. It is to be found only in the mind of the poet, and it is imagination regulated by knowledge, that enables him to form it.

JAMES BEATTIE, *Essay on Poetry and Music As They Affect the Mind*

I

SPANNING THE CENTURY—early and late—is a remarkable group of English and Scottish critics, aestheticians, and philosophers, not

---

Portions of this chapter appeared in *Johnson and His Age*, ed. James Engell (Cambridge: Harvard University Press, 1984).

major figures by the usual standards, but interesting and original in their ideas and approaches. They are enormously varied in their emphases, but generally concerned with examining and, more often than not, widening the scope of artistic inquiry. They are somewhat loosely united by a concern with the forces of the inner more than the outer life, with faculties of the mind, with beauty and power as forces of the mind, with the ways in which art is created and by which it affects an audience.

Thomas Hobbes and John Locke, already considered briefly, are certainly intellectual high priests of the movement which W. J. Bate perceptively describes as justifying "confidence in the imaginative act—an act whereby sensations, intuitions, and judgments are not necessarily retained in the memory as separate particles of knowledge to be consulted one by one, but can be coalesced and transformed into a readiness of response that is objectively receptive to the concrete process of nature and indeed actively participates in it."[1] Empirical in their orientation, strongly critical of metaphysics, they value the concrete sensation as the source of knowledge, stress combinations of sensations and associations as occasions of aesthetic pleasure, and emphasize the stimulation of imagination and emotion as the great power of a work of art. Gerald Chapman's introductory observation to what he calls the "Anglo-Scottish" section of his valuable *Literary Criticism in England, 1660–1800* is useful. The primary result of the turning-inward of empirical philosophy, he contends, "was to turn the search for laws of art into study of the laws of subjective response to it, and the laws of its origin in subjectivity." Furthermore, "since art imitates Nature," such study proceeded "to analysis of what qualities of 'objects' in Nature produce certain effects in Art." Hence we have the development of categories of effects like "sublime," "beautiful," "picturesque," "Gothic," "romantic," "magical," "faery," "pathetic."[2]

This book does not attempt a full-scale study of the Anglo-Scottish critics. Since mine is a limited thesis, what such a study would gain in comprehensiveness, it would lose in sharpness of focus and rigor of argument. The simple fact is that many of these writers are removed from questions of imitation and the new defense of literature. So, as we proceed, we shall give our attention to a significant group—Shaftesbury, James Beattie, Alexander Gerard, James Harris, Sir William Jones, Lord Kames, Hugh Blair, Robert Lowth, Adam Smith, and Thomas Twining are the major ones—who, on the one hand, are representative of the intellectual and aesthetic climate of the age and, on the other, offer fertile discussions—pro and con—that advance the continuing debate so central to this study.

This more selective process, despite its limitations, will contribute to a more vivid awareness of the new shadings given to the word "imitation" and the new force given to the defense of a more subjective literature. Granted great variation of opinion and approach, these eighteenth-century critics nevertheless remain attuned to the tradition of mimesis, to the idea, rooted in the Plato–Aristotle dialogue, that art imitates nature. At the same time new kinds of emphases, already seen in figures like Addison and Burke, begin to appear. Instead of rigid neoclassic ideas of imitation as objective representation of an ordered reality outside the mind, there is a changing view of both nature and imitation, a view that combines a more organic vision of nature with an idea of imitation more responsive to the demands of the subject. The overall effect is a widening of the scope of the imitative process to include a dynamic view of nature and a psychologically astute sense of reality that involves imagination and feeling.

II

As early as Anthony Ashley Cooper, third Earl of Shaftesbury, a philosopher–critic who in many ways exemplifies the traditionalism of neoclassicism, we can observe a more subjective view of art.[3] From a family actively involved in the politics of the age, this Shaftesbury, often in poor health, became interested in philosophy and art, and published his key ideas in the massive *Characteristics of Men, Manners, Opinions, Times* (1711). Nature for him was not simply the materials of empirical reality, but those materials touched by the mind of man, by a highly perfected taste. "A painter," he says, discussing the issue of imitation,

> if he has any genius, understands the truth and unity of design; and knows he is even then unnatural when he follows Nature too close, and strictly copies Life. For his art allows him not to bring

all nature into his piece, but a part only. However, his piece, if it be beautiful, and carries truth, must be a whole, by itself, complete, independent, and withal as great and comprehensive as he can make it [I 94].

How lyrical the dialogues of Philocles and Theocles in "The Moralists, a Philosophical Rhapsody" as they describe the primitive beauties of external nature—rough and rugged rocks and grottoes, crashing waterfalls, the terrible beauties of the deep wilderness! How pointed the comment of Theocles as he attributes this enthusiasm not just to thoughtless lovers, but to "poets, and all those other students in Nature and the arts which copy after her"! Such enthusiasm is not for the mere beauty of the moment which is but a faint shadow of a higher beauty. The rational mind must move beyond the senses in its quest for love. In a wonderfully crisp Platonic exchange the point is made without qualification: what makes the beautiful is art. " 'Tis not then the metal or matter which is beautiful with you? No. But the art? Certainly. The art then is the beauty? Right. And the art is that which beautifies? The same" (II 131).

Only the artist, the virtuoso with the innate moral sense and taste, can create the great work; "if he has not at least the idea of perfection to give him aim he will be found very defective and mean in his performance" (I 214). Such an artist probes the heart, explores the geography of the soul in his work; he imitates the inner life. Even the artist who imitates a certain outward grace and beauty seems to discover, in the midst of false manners and unrefined styles, a "true and natural one, which represents the real beauty and Venus of the kind. 'Tis the like moral grace and Venus which, discovering itself in the turns of character and the variety of human affection, is copied by the writing artist." Lacking this discovery, he can never capture the fullness of life whether he stays close to the outlines of the actual or whether he indulges a more daring and wide-ranging imagination in his representations (I 217).

In "Soliloquy: Or Advice to an Author," he develops further the theme of imitation of the inner life, using a fascinating metaphor to advance his idea of the particular mimetic quality of art and his advice as to how the artist should proceed. It is highly emotional advice for an early–eighteenth-century critic to be offering, not urging the writer to abandon an awareness of the world around us, but strongly advising him to "set afoot the powerfullest faculties of his mind, and assemble the best forces of his wit and judgment, in order to make a formal descent on the territories of the heart; resolving to decline no combat, nor hearken to any terms, till he had pierced into its inmost provinces and reached the seat of empire" (I 228–29).

Without question such an approach to the artist and his work implies a sense of art as relatively autonomous, as somewhat free from the shackles of philosophy and religion. Art for Shaftesbury, rationalist though he be, is a form of knowing, a way of giving energy to the truths of experience. The true artist, he says, can "give to an action its just body and proportions." Elevating the artist to the status of a "second *Maker*; a just Prometheus under Jove," and anticipating the organicism of Coleridge's descriptions of the secondary imagination, he sees this artist as forming "a whole, coherent and proportioned in itself, with due subjection and subordinacy of constituent parts" (I 136).[4] Still operating within the limits of a neoclassical vocabulary, Shaftesbury nevertheless—now with echoes of Plato, Plotinus, and the seventeenth-century Cambridge Platonists, and now with anticipations of the romantic critics—advances a more subjective view of the artist as man of taste and feeling and of art as expressive of the heart's penetration of the inner world. Though early in the process, he is a force in the evolution of a more personal mimesis and a more inward aesthetic.

III

There are few more thorough and more provocative discussions of imitation in eighteenth-century literary theory than Alexander Gerard's *Essay on Taste*. A Scot to the core, he was born in 1728 in Aberdeenshire, the son of a minister. After gaining his M.A. from Marischal College, Aberdeen, he went on to study theology at Aberdeen and Edinburgh, and later held the Chair of Philosophy and became Professor of Divinity at Marischal. In 1771 he became Professor of Divinity at King's College, Aberdeen. Active in philosophical circles, especially among those followers of the Common Sense philosophy opposed to the dominant empiricism of David

Hume and others, he published his influential *Essay on Taste* in 1759 and *Essay on Genius* in 1774. Gerard is clearly a major figure in what has come to be known as the Scottish intellectual Renaissance.

Gerard's *Essay on Taste*[5] especially is important to our argument for a number of reasons, but chiefly because it sees poetry as both imitative and non-imitative when measured against traditional applications of that concept. With Gerard we see a more careful distinction made between the mode of representation in the several arts and a consequent sharpening of the mimetic power of poetry. Put perhaps too crudely: poetry is not imitative if by that term we mean a kind of art—witness painting and sculpture—which represents exactly by its medium a reality beyond the mind. It is, however, even when the term seems weak and ambiguous and cries out for another, imitative in the sense that Aristotle suggests in the *Poetics*. Poetry, by its use of language, with its vagueness and at times even confusion, invades, to go back to Shaftesbury's image, the territories of the heart. It communicates not an exact, but certainly a probable, representation of the persons, actions, and attitudes of life as conceived by the poet.

The growing interiority of much eighteenth-century British criticism can be felt at the beginning of Gerard's *Essay*. "Taste," as his definition goes, "consists chiefly in the improvement of those principles which are commonly called *the powers of imagination*, and are considered by modern philosophers as *internal* or *reflex senses*, supplying us with finer and more delicate perceptions than any which can be properly referred to our external organs" (pp. 1–2). True imitations for Gerard are not copies in the familiar sense of those words. They consist not in "exactness," but in the "excellence which they represent; and the gratification which these copies afford, may almost as properly be ascribed to beauty or sublimity as to imitation" (p. 49). Granted such premisses—and we note in the above foreshadowing of Hazlitt's ideas of poetry and imitation—ordinary ideas of imitation must give way. The "rudest rocks and mountains," "objects in nature that are most deformed," "disease and pain"—we often hear echoes of Addison and Burke—these phenomena can acquire beauty when skillfully imitated in painting. As a matter of fact, he continues, it is the imitation of what are usually

54

regarded as "imperfections" and "absurdities" that can bring a deeper pleasure than mere copying of what are considered "good" and "proper." In an argument that seems at times like a modernization of Aristotle's idea of imitation leading to catharsis, and at times like Hazlitt's and Keats's view of Shakespearean tragedy as offering an intensity of representation whereby "all disagreeables evaporate," he addresses himself to Shakespeare as illustrating his point:

> A perfect imitation of characters morally evil, can make us dwell with pleasure on them, notwithstanding the uneasy sentiments of disapprobation and abhorrence which they excite. The character of Iago is detestable, but we admire Shakespear's representation of it. Nay, imperfect and mixt characters are, in all kinds of writing, preferred to faultless ones, as being juster copies of real nature. The pleasant sensation resulting from the imitation is so intense, that it overpowers and converts into delight even the *uneasy* impressions which spring from the objects imitated [p. 51].

Gerard is one of several critics and literary theorists who, in challenging poetry's right to be called imitative, actually proceed to redefine imitation, to recast Aristotle's idea in eighteenth-century terms. In the process two things stand out: (*a*) a widening of the objects of imitation; and (*b*) a more psychologically sophisticated consideration and defense of the particular ways by which poetic imitation is carried out. Painting and sculpture are seen as the "most perfect" imitations because, on an obvious level, they produce the "most perfect likeness" (p. 53). The struggle of history painting to capture a significant subject while "representing passion and character by figure and colour" is a sure sign of its skill in overcoming difficulties and achieving beauty. In this sense poetry is "more imperfectly mimetic" than the other arts, "imitating by instituted symbols, no wise resembling things" (p. 55); yet in this very imperfection reside its peculiar merit, its uniqueness, its power to engage the heart and draw it to a more intense perception of reality.

Ironically, in its imperfection lies its superiority. In a statement all the more remarkable given its mid-century date, Gerard does not avoid the term "mimetic" and adopt a new one like "expressive," but rather gives a new shape and fullness to the old Aristotelian term. The superiority of poetry to all its sister arts, he argues, "is its peculiar and unrivalled power of imitating the noblest and most important of all subjects, the calmest sentiments of the heart, and human characters displayed in a long series of conduct." The premiss underlying this claim for the superiority of poetry is not just "the excellencies of the *instruments* or *manners* of imitation" claimed by all the sister arts, "but also the moment of what they imitate, and the value of the *ends* to which they are adapted" (p. 55). Gerard lends greater complexity to this question of what are the objects of imitation. Far from simply men in action, from the universe without, the universe within is a major concern. The representation of a psychologically rich experience, blending things new and natural, enlightened by the power of fiction and a rich variety of imagery is poetry's unique claim to excellence, and such a claim is central to the new defense of poetry.

In the appendix to the essay called "Concerning the Question, Whether Poetry be properly an Imitative Art? and if it be, In what sense is it Imitative?" Gerard cites Aristotle as the father of the idea of poetry as imitation, and complains about the lack of any clear definition or description of the nature of this imitation. He further cites those contemporary theorists like Lord Kames who deny that poetry is imitative, arguing only for painting and sculpture. These other arts capture the form and shape of visible objects, and communicate the resemblance to the appropriate senses. Even dramatic poetry may be considered properly imitative, not simply describing, but exhibiting conversations and actions. Lyric poetry—where "the poet, in his own person, describes or relates," where the urgency of emotion is expressed—presents the problem. Here the poet struggles with language in order to articulate the complex rhythms of the heart. Such language, such signs, of course, "bear no resemblance to the things signified by them; and therefore the poem can have no proper resemblance to the thing described in it" (pp. 277–78).

Yet poetry is imitative if in a quite different and striking way, the way in which painting of a certain kind is.

> But suppose that a painter, instead of copying an individual object with which he is acquainted, invents a subject; suppose, for

instance, that he paints an Hercules, from a standard idea in his own mind: in this case, the picture is not an imitation, as being a copy or resemblance of any one individual existing in nature. It is still an imitation, but in a quite different sense: the subject itself is an imitation; it is, not a real individual, but a general representation of the make of a strong man. The imitation made by poetry, is of this very kind. The poet conceives his subject; and this subject is an imitation; it is not, in all its circumstances, a thing which really exists in nature, or a fact which has really happened; it only resembles things which exist, or which have happened [pp. 280–81].

Gerard builds solidly on the Aristotelian distinction between history, things as they are, and poetry, things as they may be. Poetry represents the probable; the poet, in imagining his subject, is, in that very action, imitating. Like many other theorists of the time, Gerard will often use the term "description" to suggest more precisely the imitation of the inner life. He consistently separates mere adherence to the real thing, accompanied by fanciful, adorning imagery, from that which is most distinctive of true poetry: namely, its simultaneity with the processes of nature. This is surely the kind of defense of literature to be seen in force fifty years later in the criticism of Wordsworth and Coleridge. "In a word," says Gerard, "poetry is called an imitation, not because it produces a lively idea of its immediate subject, but because this subject itself is an imitation of some part of real nature" (p. 283).

It is what the interior universe of the artist brings to the world outside that constitutes great art. It is the imagination of the artist which invents, which creates the language, signs, symbols which may not have a resemblance to the subject described but which excite "an idea of the object described, as conceived by the poet" (p. 277.) In the *Iliad* Homer

only takes his hints from the real events of the Trojan war; he introduces the heroes who served in it; but he engages them in whatever combats he thinks proper; he feigns those circumstances, those turns of success, and those consequences of the several combats, which produce the best effects on the imagination and the passions. . . . The subject of every poem, is to a certain degree a *fable*; and to the very same degree, it is an imitation [p. 283].

Sounding now like Aristotle and now like Addison, Alexander Gerard, philosopher–literary theorist of the Scottish Renaissance, argues for poetry as a special kind of imitation, with a new and lively flavor in his approach. If a close rendering of external reality is the business of true imitative art, then poetry does not qualify. If describing the shadings of human emotion as they are caught by the suggestive and illuminating power of language and imagery is seen as mimetic of vital dimensions of reality, then poetry is a vital form of imitation. If great art imitates nature, and the geography of the spirit is part of that nature, what else but poetry can capture the windings of the spirit so well? Gerard has taken the idea of imitation in a new direction, and in the process has justified a literature more subjective but no less real.

IV

James Beattie, celebrated author of the exuberantly romantic poem *The Minstrel,* and a professor of philosophy at Marischal College, Aberdeen, is also important as a literary theorist who contributes to the continuing discussion of the imitative aspect of art and to the defense of a new kind of poetry. Although not as direct as some of his contemporaries in his references to Aristotelian themes, he nevertheless reveals a full awareness of these themes. In his most famous work, *Essays: On Poetry and Music As They Affect the Mind; On Laughter, and Ludicrous Composition; On the Usefulness of Classical Learning* (1779), he stresses, in the tradition of neoclassical criticism, the teaching and pleasing functions of literature, but goes on to distinguish sharply poetry from history and philosophy.[6] Unlike philosophers and historians, "the poet must do a greater deal for the sake of pleasure only; and if he fail to please, he may indeed deserve praise on other accounts, but as a poet, he has done nothing" (pp. 9–10). Indeed pleasure communicated through the engagement of the inner life is the vehicle through which poetry achieves its unique educative power. Poetry is not concerned with "merely the communication of moral and physical truth." "Whatever tends to raise those human affections that are favourable to truth and virtue, or to repress the opposite passions, will always gratify and improve our moral and intellectual powers" (p. 19).

Beattie grounds his idea of imitation in this emphasis on pleasure as a central purpose of poetry. Since we do not derive pleasure from the unnatural, he argues, poetry must proceed in accordance with nature. But it must not simply duplicate nature; it must, without distorting the essential, see its more vital meanings in new ways. In so doing, it is more pleasurable because we grant greater freedom to its fictions and modes of expression, and "consequently that poetry must be, not according to real nature, but according to nature improved to that degree, which is consistent with probability, and suitable to the poet's purpose. And hence it is that we call Poetry, AN IMITATION OF NATURE." An "imitation," properly so called, has within it something not in the original. "If the prototype and transcript be exactly alike, if there be nothing in the one which is not in the other; we call the latter a representation, a copy, a draught, or a picture of the former; but we may never call it an imitation" (pp. 86–87). Music, unlike poetry, is not properly an imitative art since it does not imitate a particular part of nature. Only when it readily puts one in mind of the thing imitated can art be called imitative (p. 129).

Beattie continues the widening of the concept of imitation already noted, and, in so doing, seems to anticipate romantic manifestos. In a passage cataloguing the objects of imitation—a passage that underlines the quest of art for "the highest possible perfection"—he pays a great deal of attention to the representation of the inner life. Poetical representations, he says, must rival the highest excellence they are capable of achieving. External nature must be more picturesque; action more vigorous; "sentiments more expressive of the feelings and character, and more suitable to the circumstances of the speaker" (p. 54). This pattern of perfection is to be found, not in real nature, the territory of history, but only in the mind of the poet, ultimately to be shaped by an informed imagination. The poet, in addressing the reader, in trying to evoke joy or sorrow, admiration or terror, to exhibit a Venus or Tisiphone, an Achilles or Thersites, a dance or a battle, "generally copies an idea of his own imagination, an idea rooted in concrete experience" (p. 56). What Beattie is doing is stressing an older emphasis on poetry's attempt to capture the universal in the particular and, in so doing, to complete nature, including in that universal an area of life—emotional, imaginative—often neglected in previous and even contemporary discussions.

With this new emphasis on the imitation of feelings comes the question of how this imitation is best carried out, of how the geography of the spirit can best be traversed and mapped. Beattie, like many of his eighteenth-century colleagues, stresses the power of "tropes and figures" to communicate the complex nuances of human response (p. 265). The language of poetry must be "an imitation of the language of Nature" (p. 193), of "human speech, not in that imperfect state wherein it is used on the common occasions of life, but in that state of perfection, whereof, consistently with verisimilitude, it may be supposed to be susceptible" (p. 195). In a wonderfully lyrical passage Beattie describes the freedom of the true poet in his imitations. Sounding somewhat like Wordsworth in the Preface to the *Lyrical Ballads*, he sees the poet as subject to no restraints save general truth. The demands of a narrow literal truth are absent as the poet seeks to please his reader only by "an appeal to his sensibility and imagination." The poet's imagination "is therefore continually at work, ranging through the whole of real and probable existence, 'glancing from heaven to earth, from earth to heaven,' in quest of images and ideas suited to the emotions he himself feels, and to the sympathies he would communicate to others" (pp. 266–67).

Beattie uses two striking literary examples to point up his emphasis on the imitation of the inner life in poetry. In these examples, we can observe a strong suggestion of a theory of the lyric with emphasis on the speaker, state of mind, and the nature of expression. He considers Anacreon, the Greek lyric poet, and Thomas Gray's eloquent bard in the poem of the same name, and treats them as speakers of their respective poems. Anacreon warbles his songs in the midst of flowers, his mind and spirit indolent and caught up in objects of his pleasure. Gray's bard, surrounded by the sublime desolation of mountains and streams, curses Edward I, persecutor of bards, and, caught up in fits of passions, prophesies disaster for the king and his descendants. "If perspicuity and simplicity," says Beattie in comparing the two lyric voices, "be natural in the images of Anacreon, as they certainly are, a figurative style and desultory composition are no less natural in this inimitable performance of Gray" (p. 269).

In Beattie and other critics of the age, there is an interest in the character of the poet, to be sure—the intensity of his feelings, the activity of his imagination, the depth of his sympathy with nature. There is further a new, and profoundly psychological, concern with the audience. In the good work of art, the poet, by his figured representation of strong feeling, must of necessity draw his audience closer to the external and internal universe, must provoke them to feel the beauties of sea, sky, mountain, to share sympathetically joy and sorrow, exaltation and pain, and consequently to widen their range of awareness so that their perspectives are broadened and their spirit illuminated. In language that strongly suggests Hazlitt's idea of gusto, Beattie argues that if the true poet would move "the passions and sympathies of mankind," his own must be moved, that many passions, by their very nature, "increase the activity of the imagination" (pp. 266–67). In provoking them thus, the poet is truly an educative force in society, and his art is moral in the noblest sense. To share intensely the condition of another person, whether it be pleasurable or painful, is healthful and constructive. "Hence the good of others becomes in some measure our good, and their evil our evil; the obvious effect of which is to bind men more closely together in society, and prompt them to promote the good, and relieve the distresses, of one another" (p. 193).

James Beattie, a lyric poet himself, brings a strongly subjective dimension to his concept of imitation, widening it to include a whole new area of interest in the workings of the mind and feelings. He further develops a way of talking about lyric poetry that attends to the artist's shaping of the demands of the inner life in a richly imaginative language and to the audience's sympathetic response to the creations of art.

V

Richard Hurd, for twenty-eight years bishop of Worcester and celebrated chiefly for his pioneering justification of the Gothic in his *Letters on Chivalry and Romance*, needs also to be considered in any treatment of the shifting focus of imitation in eighteenth-century literary theory. He is indeed one of a company of theorists, respectful of more classical aesthetics, but eager to defend romantic ways of thinking about literature. A classical scholar of note, Hurd edited Horace's *Ars Poetica* in 1794 and the *Epistola ad Augustum* in 1751. To the latter he added "A Discourse Concerning Poetical Imitation." Another essay of importance—"A Letter to Mason, on the Marks of Imitation"—appeared in 1757.

Hurd is quite specific in his ways of talking about imitation.[7] In "Dissertation III on Poetical Imitation," he cites Aristotle as he talks of poetry as "the noblest and most extensive of the mimetic arts; having all creation for its object, and ranging the entire circuit of universal being" (p. 111). Interesting in this rather staightforward statement is the emphasis on a range of imitation, on poetry's world as an extensive and inclusive wealth of universal being. Hurd proceeds to amplify on this matter of the breadth of poetry's concern as he outlines the materials over which the active imagination of the poet travels. There is, of course, the material world. But—and this is more significant for our purposes in this essay—there is a strong focus on the poet, on the *"internal workings of his own mind, under which I comprehend the manners, sentiments, and passions,"* or, moving beyond poetry, on *"those internal operations, that are made objective to sense by the outward signs of gesture, attitude, or action"* (pp. 115–16).

In this area of imitating, "in imitating the *marks* of vigorous affection," writers differ considerably. The challenge is great. The artist must capture not only the wondrous variety of the world around him, but also the vast complexity and richness of the world within. Hurd has widened the circumference of nature to include external and internal reality as well as the interaction of the two. Great art must explore the subjective as well as the objective if it is to fulfill its chief mission of imitation. The movements of the inner life, if not visible to the eye, are no less real than *"permanent, external existences"*; "to succeed in this work of painting the *signatures of internal affection*, requires a larger experience, or quicker penetration, than copying after still life" (p. 148).

Lest he be seen as advancing the idea of a highly subjective, idiosyncratic form of imitation and of art, he is careful, in a summing-up statement like the following, to stress the classical notion of the persistence of the subjects of great art, extending those subjects, however, to include not just significant human actions but also large human emotions that do not change essentially over the centuries. Anticipating the romantic idea of the creative imagination, he stresses the power of mind. Experience, he says, provides the materials of imitation just as it provides the stuff of human knowledge, but "it is in the *operations* of the mind upon them, that the glory of *poetry*, as of *science*, consists" (pp. 176–77).

Just as in his *Letters on Chivalry and Romance* he bemoaned the loss of a world of "fine fabling" in the more realistic and rationalistic literature and criticism of his time and vigorously supported the emotional and imaginative power of the Gothic, so in his essays on imitation he sought to include this world of imaginative wealth among the glories of artistic representation. The mind, in its search for gratification, seeks more than a view of the external world, seeks a world touched by its imaginings. Pleasure comes ultimately from activity of mind, and it is this activity that the best poetry stimulates. As he puts it, in a graphic language and imagery that seems to look ahead to the later *Discourses* of Sir Joshua Reynolds, pleasure "is the ultimate and appropriate end of poetry." But, unlike other kinds of writing which are under the control of reason and which *"buckle and bow the mind to the nature of things,"* poetry "accommodates itself to the desires of the mind," and seeks to "gratify" those desires. For pleasure, he contends, comes not from the calm recognition of some objective idea or beauty beyond the self, but from the engagement of the mind by a recognition in a work of art of what it passionately seeks but cannot completely find in the ordinary business of living. Poetry does indeed gratify the mind's desires, but in a vitally unique way, a way that challenges and outdistances the ways of philosophy, history, and other forms of knowledge (pp. 3–4).

In Richard Hurd's remarks on artistic imitation, we note an emerging romantic theory of literature. Whether studying the imitative dimension of poetry or the power of art to capture a world of imaginative adventure, he is consistently stressing the psychological, the energy of the mind's resources to bring color and strength to life and, most especially, to art.

VI

Lest one feel that there is anything like a consensus on the idea of imitation among the eighteenth-century Anglo-Scottish critics, it might be useful to look at a number of them with either different shadings of opinion or in some cases with what appear to be strongly negative reactions to any suggestion that poetry is, in Aristotle's terms, imitative. To several, the chief objection is rooted in the idea that any genuine imitation must have a natural resemblance to the thing imitated. Hence poetry, with the fertile but ambivalent medium of language, cannot match the immediacy of sculpture and painting which evoke the objects of imitation more directly. Often the activity of poetry is described as "description," and the effect created is called "sympathy," although from the contexts in which the words are used, it seems relatively clear that these words represent an attempt to give more scope to the term "imitation," that they reveal the critic's struggle to come to terms with a widening of human consciousness and the need to represent it. Hugh Blair in *Lectures on Rhetoric and Belles Lettres* is a good example.[8] Born in 1718, Blair is part of a Scottish literary circle that included David Hume and Adam Smith. A minister noted for his sermons, he was also a professor of rhetoric at the University of Edinburgh whose rhetorical writings were enormously influential during the century in England and America.

Citing both Aristotle and Addison as sources in his *Lectures*—examples of both classical and romantic views of imitation—Blair complains of the lack of precision in contemporary critical language and contends that "Neither discourse in general, nor poetry in particular, can be called altogether imitative arts" (p. 94). The distinction between "Imitation" and "Description" must be made. Sounding very much like Addison on the pleasures of imagination, he argues that poetry derives its great power from "significancy of words" (p. 96). The power, however, is one of description, not of imitation, description being "the raising in the mind the conception of an object by means of some arbitrary or instituted symbols, understood only by those who agree in the institution of them; such are words and writing" (p. 94). In another treatise, *A Critical Dissertation on the Poems of Ossian*,[9] Blair, an ardent supporter and defender of James Macpherson's wildly romantic Ossian poetry, stresses the power of primitive poetry to capture "the most natural pictures of ancient manners." What these pictures offer is not simply an historical account—surely a less valuable record—but "the history of human imagination and passion." Such a history provokes sympathy, makes us "acquainted with the notions and feelings of our fellow creatures in the most artless ages" (p. 1).

VII

The same kinds of reservations about a more traditional conception of imitation can be found in Henry Home, Lord Kames in his celebrated *Elements of Criticism*. A judge in Edinburgh for many years, Kames wrote on topics from law to history to ethics. His *Elements of Criticism* was an attempt to construct a full-blown aesthetics, and the work was widely read in Scotland, on the Continent, and in America.[10]

Connecting criticism to the heart as well as the head, Kames sees his principles as drawn "from human nature." Like Blair, he regards only painting and sculpture as by their very nature imitative (I 16). "Language," he says, "has no archetype in nature, more than music or architecture; unless where, like music, it is imitative of sound or motion" (II 234). Sounding again like Addison on the secondary pleasures of imagination—those pleasures not in bodies but in the mind—he contrasts the order and regularity of beauty with the ruggedness and power of grandeur and sublimity. The latter "generally signify the quality or circumstance in the objects by which the emotions are produced; sometimes the emotions themselves" (I 226). Using the word "description" as a matter of course, and using it to suggest a more wide-ranging kind of representation, he praises the power of art, of language, to convey more than reality itself. Vivid and accurate description raises ideas no less distinct. "I have not words to describe this act, other than that I perceive the thing as a spectator, and as existing in any presence" (I 108). Language, never completely adequate to the great task of evoking a sense of reality, of what Kames calls "ideal presence," has, nevertheless, a power to suggest in the mind the nuances of experience often not apparent in a matter-of-fact account. It yields up the riches of creation in a way history cannot. In offering lively and distinct images, it stirs the reader's passions by throwing him into "a kind of reverie, in which state, losing the consciousness of self and of reading, his present occupation, he conceives every incident as passing in his presence precisely as if he were an eyewitness" (I 112).

Built into Kames's aesthetic of representation is a new defense of fiction, of art in general. Not merely a fanciful creation, not simply an adorning of everyday experience, art holds meaning in the confines of its language and imagery. Man's intellectual faculties can take him a distance, but they lack that quality of sympathy which enables him to enter into and share the fullness of experience. They simply cannot "dive far even into his own nature" (I 105). Only the emotions, the faculties addressed by the fictions of art, can confront the complexity of human experience and convey a sense of ideal presence. Language, "by means of fiction, has the command of our sympathy for the good of others. By the same means, our sympathy may also be raised for our own good." For Kames no other discipline does more to make virtue habitual, to drive its truth home not just to the head, but to the heart—to the full range of human awareness. Fiction holds a power over the mind that affords "an endless variety of refined amusement," and such amusement "is a fine resource in solitude; and by sweetening the temper, improves society" (I 126–27).

Kames's formulation of a more sensuous aesthetic stressing poetry's special form of imitation and its special mode of driving home the truth of experience is still another example of the movement of eighteenth-century literary theory toward greater subjectivity, toward justifying the emotions themselves as a significant part of reality and hence worthy of representation in the work of art.

VIII

Sir William Jones, one of the great scholars of the age, a linguist fluent in thirteen languages and a specialist in Oriental languages and literatures, was the author of two striking essays appended to his *Poems, Consisting Chiefly of Translations from the Asiatic Languages* (1772).[11]

66

One of them, "On the Arts Commonly Called Imitative," is especially important for our purposes, taking the position, as it does, that "though poetry and music have, certainly, a power of imitating the manners of men and several objects in nature, yet . . . their greatest effect is not produced by imitation, but by a very different principle, which must be sought for in the deepest recesses of the human mind" (pp. 872–73). Here again we see the theorist challenging the Aristotelian mimetic designation and posing the problem of the inwardness of poetry. The artist is not so much an imitator of nature as the voice of nature itself, and the true subject matter of poetry is the inner life, passion and sympathy. Consequently, Jones is primarily concerned with lyric poetry, with the Song of Solomon, the prophets, the lyrics of Alcaeus, Alcman, and Ibycus, the hymns of Callimachus, the elegy of Moschus on Bion—with a kind of poetry where there is no real imitation as Aristotle conceived it. Even though some kinds of painting are strictly imitative in that they capture exactly in line and color their subjects, the greatest pictures—the various representations of the Crucifixion, Domenichino's painting of the martyrdom of St. Agnes—"cannot be said to imitate, [rather their] most powerful influence over the mind arises, like that of the other arts, from sympathy" (p. 879).

Like other critics in this chapter, Jones is puzzled by the challenge of dealing with a new problem: how to designate a poetry that represents not the world around us but that within us, how to find a vocabulary that will enable one to talk about the lyric. Grounded in the classics and in the classical views of Aristotle, he cannot, at least on the surface, think of lyric poetry as imitative. Words and sounds "have no kind of resemblance to visible objects; and what is an imitation but a resemblance of some other thing" (p. 879)? This is a line taken by several other critics. At the same time, however, Jones is keenly aware of the power of the inner life and the need to represent it in poetry. What results is not so much the rejection of the idea of imitation as the search for language to describe more adequately the representation of passion, especially in lyric poetry. Predictably the two most common words are "description" and "sympathy," and the approach taken is very much that of Addison when discussing the secondary pleasures of the imagination. One cannot help noticing in his analysis of the process that he is struggling to deal with how, psychologically, feeling is communicated by the artist and received by the audience. What is being expressed, it would seem, is an aesthetic of imitation as it relates to the inner life, an aesthetic that might be described as follows: (a) Since the emotions are vital aspects of human life, art must represent them; (b) but such emotions do not lend themselves to the kind of direct imitation that one might find in painting and sculpture; (c) therefore, strong and vital language and imagery are needed to trigger in the minds of the audience an awareness of and a sympathy with the feelings expressed.

In a fascinating section at the end of his essay, Jones argues for the superiority of imitation by sympathy to imitation by exact description. Such exact description—not that description already considered in this essay—he contends, is "the meanest part" of both poetry and music, for true imitation lies in resemblance not duplication. He then creates a scene in which a poet, a musician, and a painter are attempting to convey to a friend or patron the pleasure each has felt at the sight of a beautiful prospect. The poet "will form an agreeable assemblage of lively images which he will express in smooth and elegant verses of a sprightly measure; he will describe the most delightful objects, and will add to the graces of his description a certain delicacy of sentiment, and a spirit of cheerfulness" (p. 880). The musician will similarly create strong effects by utilizing the many resources of his medium. The painter will, by the very nature of his medium, fall short of his competitors; his pencil may "express a simple passion," but "cannot paint a thought or draw the shades of sentiment" (p. 880). The painter can, however, achieve his own success with graceful and elegant landscapes, rich and glowing colors, striking perspective, and great variety. Summing up the argument that emerges from his imaginary competition, he says:

> the finest parts of poetry, music, and painting are expressive of the passions, and operate on our minds by sympathy; . . . the inferior parts of them are descriptive of natural objects, and affect us chiefly by substitution; . . . the expressions of love, pity, desire, and the tender passions, as well as the descriptions of objects that delight the senses, produce in the arts what we call the beautiful; . . . hate, anger, fear, and the terrible passions, as well as objects

which are unpleasing to the senses, are productive of the sublime when they are aptly expressed or described [p. 881].

Once again—this time in Jones—we see the strong emphasis on poetry, as well as other art, as conveyor of the passions. The finest art moves beyond mere duplication to suggest the possibilities of nature and to draw readers and spectators to those possibilities with a strong and genuine sympathy. Language, with its indeterminacy, with its vast range of suggestiveness, can capture most successfully the complex and rich nuances of human emotion and bring the reader into a more intimate and sympathetic relationship with that emotion.

IX

In James Harris (1709–1780), whose uncle was the Earl of Shaftesbury, we find still another eighteenth-century figure who pursues questions of aesthetics in new and interesting ways. After graduating from Wadham College, Oxford, he pursued legal studies at Lincoln's Inn, acted as magistrate for the County of Wiltshire, and later served as a lord of the Admiralty (1762), a lord of the Treasury (1763), and Secretary and Comptroller to the Queen (1774). He wrote in the course of his career on a variety of topics—philosophical, philological, literary, ethical, aesthetic—but it is the aesthetic which concerns us here.

In 1774 Harris published his *Three Treatises*: I. *Concerning Art.* II. *Concerning Music, Painting, and Poetry.* III. *Concerning Happiness*.[12] In the first two treatises Harris conducts a systematic examination of the foundation of art, an account of its manifestations in the media of music, painting, and poetry, a detailed analysis of the mimetic power of poetry, and a defense of its moral force in society. In the first treatise, dedicated to Shaftesbury and using the techniques of the aesthetic dialogue so often employed by the philosopher, the speakers agree on a wide-ranging subject matter for art. "If this, continued he, be true, it should seem that the common or universal subject of art was, all those contingent natures which lie within the reach of the human powers to influence.—I acknowledge, said I, it appears so" (p. 11). In an extraordinary statement, remarkably Aristotelian in its force, the speakers agree on the final cause of art—a cause neither didactic nor aesthetic. In language that suggests art's power to do more than entertain or instruct in the narrow senses of those words, to rival nature and hence to reveal it in its essential outlines, the dialogue proceeds. The first speaker argues that art is created and all its operations are brought to bear by " 'the want or absence of something appearing good; relative to human life, and attainable by man, but superior to his natural and uninstructed faculties.' " And the second speaker quickly agrees that "the account appeared probable" (pp. 16–17). In short, art holds within itself the power to compete with and outdo ordinary reality, to represent things not just as they are, but as they ought to be if the full range of human possibility could be brought to bear.

In the second treatise, still in an Aristotelian vein, Harris moves at once to a consideration of imitation. As with all the critics we have been considering, there is a clear assumption that the informed reader is familiar with the several classical and neoclassical assumptions about imitation. There is also a desire to push forward, to explore all shadings of those assumptions, to advance a contemporary view of imitation responsive to the realities of nature and the psychological complexity of the human person. Again the force of Addison's views on imitation seems a strong one. First, there is the emphasis on sensation, on the mind's being "made conscious of the natural world and its affections, and of other minds and their affections, by the several organs of the senses." Then there is the widening of the process of imitation; the arts of music, painting, and poetry "imitate either parts or affections of this natural world, or else the passions, energies, and other affections of mind." These arts, then, are "all mimetic or imitative," and differ only as they imitate by different media: "painting and music, by media which are natural; poetry, for the greatest part, by a medium which is artificial" (p. 28).

Poetry, according to Harris, has up to this time received attention for "mere natural resemblance" (p. 33), an inferior form of imitation, and one that is carried off better by painting and music. Poetry's medium of words renders it "less similar, less immediate, and less intelligible" than painting (p. 35), and yet poetry aspires to rival the imitations of painting and music. Language, for all its inadequacies, is the magical medium to convey the complex rhythms of human feeling. Actually "in manners and passions there is no other which can exhibit them to us after that clear, precise, and definite way, as they in nature stand allotted to the various sorts of men, and are found to constitute the several characters of each" (p. 38). For Harris poetry is "much superior to either of the other mimetic arts," equally excellent in the accuracy of its imitation" and in its "subjects which far surpass, as well in utility, as in dignity" (p. 39).

X

Certainly one of the most interesting pieces of literary history and criticism in the eighteenth century is the *Lectures on the Sacred Poetry of the Hebrews* (1753) by Bishop Robert Lowth.[13] It is, of course, a splendid example of a concern with ancient religious poetry as illustrative of those qualities of spontaneity and sublimity that tend to be minimized in more polished and sophisticated eras. It also reveals a new consideration of the Old Testament more as a poetic text than as a narrowly religious document. Lowth, born in 1710, succeeded Joseph Spence in the prestigious Oxford Chair of Poetry in 1741. The lectures on a variety of topics from imagination to allegory, to the sublimity of the Old Testament, to ideas of the lyric were collected in his *Lectures*, a work for which Oxford gave him an honorary degree a year after its publication. The *magnum opus* of this scholar, clergyman, and member of the Royal Society, originally written in Latin, was translated into English in 1787, and became very influential.

For Lowth poetry, in accordance with Aristotle's definition in the *Poetics*, is at root an imitation, although the matter imitated is as varied as *Oedipus the King* and The Book of Job. Like many other theorists, Lowth sees poetry as the imitation not just of actions, but of emotions, not just of the deeds of great heroes but of the inner turmoil of God's creatures. So strong is the emphasis on the expression of emotion that M. H. Abrams groups him with his expressive tradition of criticism, constructing a line from Lowth to John Keble and ultimately to Herder, who claimed Lowth as his source in his *Vom Geist der ebraischen Poesie*, published in 1782.[14]

Abrams is, of course, quite right to see the expressive dimension of Lowth's criticism, although it is, I think, more fruitful to see what we might call the amplification of the mimetic in his reading of Aristotelian terminology and his eventual formulation of a distinctive idea of imitation that connects him with his eighteenth-century heritage and prepares the way for the romantics.

An interesting starting point in our discussion is Lowth's Lecture XXXIII, "The Poem of Job Not a Perfect Drama." Using Aristotle's theory of tragedy as a springboard, he proceeds to compare *Oedipus the King* and The Book of Job—one thoroughly Greek and the other thoroughly Hebrew—to illustrate the former's emphasis on plot and action, and the latter's on character and emotion. The documents selected are suggestive not simply because one is more expressive than the other, but because in moving from one to the other, one can see the range of experience—from the external to the internal; from men in action to men in inner turmoil—which Lowth finds in Aristotle's idea of nature. Although the parallel is by no means exact, we cannot help being reminded of the brilliant opening chapter in Erich Auerbach's *Mimesis: The Representation of Reality in Western Literature* with its analysis of the recognition scene in Book 19 of Homer's *Odyssey* (in which the housekeeper Euryclea knows Odysseus by the scar on his thigh and keeps the secret from nearby Penelope) and the sacrifice of Isaac in Genesis 22:1.[15] Auerbach, also a student of imitation, sees in the two texts splendid illustrations of two different ways of representing reality: one more realistic, the other more inward; one more direct, the other more suggestive. Unlike *Oedipus,* argues Lowth in his analysis, The Book of Job contains no plot or action, as Aristotle would define them; it deals with a state of soul. It contains no change of fortune for its central character, but rather "a representation of those manners, passions and sentiments, which might actually be expected in such a situation" (p. 276).

Lowth's greatest emphasis is on the sublimity of Hebrew poetry— not merely a sublimity of "objects" charged by powerful imagery and diction, "but that force of composition, whatever it be, which strikes and overpowers the mind, which excites the passions, and which expresses ideas at once with perspicuity and elevation" (pp. 112–13). Taking Longinus as his guide, he focuses sharply on poetry

72

as revelatory of intense feeling and on language as the strong conduit of that feeling. He distinguishes between "the language of reason" with its care and clarity and "the language of passions" which is completely different; "the conceptions burst out into a turbid stream, expressive in a manner of the internal conflict; the more vehement break out in hasty confusion; they catch (without search or study) whatever is impetuous, vivid, or energetic" (p. 113).

Whereas the mind speaks straightforwardly and literally, the passions express themselves poetically. With great psychological concern he describes the mind when impassioned as struggling to get beyond some kind of exact or literal mode of expression and to find one agreeable to its sensations, more able to communicate concretely the urgency and depth of its feelings. The passions "are naturally inclined to amplification; they wonderfully magnify and exaggerate whatever dwells upon the mind, and labor to express it in animated, bold, and magnificent terms" (p. 113). This expression may take one of two forms. The first is the old-fashioned method of imagery illustrating the subject. The other, more in keeping with the new turning-inward of literary and psychological theory, employs "new and extraordinary forms of expression, which are indeed possessed of great force and efficacy in this respect especially, that they in some degree imitate or represent the present habit and state of the soul" (p. 113). Interestingly, the words "imitate" and "represent" are stressed as is the "state of the soul." Art is for Lowth, the historian and critic of ancient Hebrew poetry, still an imitation, although the subject matter has become increasingly personal and although language by its very indeterminacy is the great vehicle for communicating the wealth of possibility in the inner life of man.

XI

No study of eighteenth-century literary theory can be complete if it neglects the work of Adam Smith, known perhaps best for his revolutionary economic treatise *The Wealth of Nations*, but also crucial for an understanding of an entire range of critical issues in the age. Born in Glasgow and educated at the University and later at Oxford, he went on to lecture at Edinburgh where he knew important philosophers like Lord Kames and David Hume. For twelve years he was Professor of Logic at the University of Glasgow, a time during which he wrote his celebrated philosophical treatise *The Theory of Moral Sentiments* (1759). In this we find his pioneering work on psychological response to the arts, especially on the concept of the sympathetic imagination so central to the romantic theory of Hazlitt and Keats.

Smith was also interested in the foundation of the arts, and particularly in the imitative dimension, as can be seen in a remarkable piece "Of the Nature of that Imitation which takes place in what are called The Imitative arts" in his *Essays on Philosophical Subjects*.[16] Imitation is the heart of the creative process, according to Smith, and close resemblance is not the best kind of imitation. Although the copy may derive some merit from its reminder of an original, "an original can certainly derive none from the resemblance of its copy" (p. 178). Poetry, with its powerful vehicle of language, can express many things fully and distinctly which Dance can catch only imperfectly, things "such as the reasonings and judgments of the understanding; the ideas, fancies, and suspicions of the imagination; the sentiments, emotions, and passions of the heart" (p. 189).

Music, however, has a special imitative power, to be matched by none of the other arts. It, of course, strives to make a thing of one kind resemble something of a different kind, shaping and bending as it does the measure and melody so as to capture, on the one hand, the special tone and language of conversation and, on the other, the special accents and styles of emotion and passion. But the power of music and words in expressing strong passion outdoes every form of discourse which lacks the special graces of music. "Neither Prose nor Poetry," he says, "can venture to imitate those almost endless repetitions of passion." They may describe, but they do not fully imitate. The music of a passionate air, however, frequently does, "and it never makes its way so directly or so irresistibly to the heart as when it does so" (pp. 191–92).

Smith has less to say about the imitative aspects of poetry than many of the others we have been considering, and he is sharp in his elevation of music as in some ways the greatest of the imitative arts. He is, however, important for our purposes in this chapter, and indeed in the overall context of this book, in that he represents a

74

major eighteenth-century philosopher interested in how the arts imitate and setting down, in an important essay on the subject, the special power of art to capture the complexity of the emotional life and to render it in unique ways. If poetry must at times yield the palm to music, it does so as a happy collaborator, a willing contributor to a fuller representation of reality.

XII

Little is known about Thomas Twining beyond the information supplied by editors of his work. A fellow of Sidney Sussex at Cambridge University, a clergyman and rector of St. Mary's in Colchester, a devotee of literature and music, a classical scholar praised by contemporaries, he produced his most celebrated work, *Aristotle's Treatise on Poetry, Translated, With Two Dissertations, on Poetical and Musical Imitation*, in 1789.[17]

As an end-of-the century theorist, Twining is especially interesting as he looks back on the writings of other critics. His aim, he tells us, is to clear up a gathering confusion brought about by the writings of many of the critics we have been considering. Like the schoolmaster, he sets out at once, in the first dissertation, entitled "On Poetry, Considered as an Imitative Art," to make distinctions between proper and improper uses of the term "imitation." In its proper sense, it must meet two conditions: "the resemblance must be immediate; i.e. between the *imitation, or imitative work itself,* and the object imitated; and it must also be *obvious.*" In sculpture, painting, mimicry, voice, gesture, "the resemblance is *obvious;* we recognize the object imitated; and it is, also, *immediate*—it lies in the imitative *work,* or *energy, itself;* or in other words, in the very materials, or *sensible media,* by which the imitation is conveyed. All *these* copies, therefore, are called strictly and intelligibly imitations" (I 4–5).

With poetry the situation is different. Here words are the medium, and, strictly speaking, they imitate only to the extent that there is a resemblance of "words considered as mere SOUND, to the *sounds* and *motions* of the objects imitated." In a wider sense, however, with words as medium, "the resemblance is so faint and distant and of so general and vague a nature, that it would never, *of itself,*

75

lead us to recognize the object imitated. We discover not the *likeness* till we know the *meaning*" (1 5–6). The relationship of word and thing is arbitrary or conventional, then; much depends on certain qualities of suggestiveness in the language. Such resemblances, however delicate and suggestive, "are yet a source of real beauties, of beauties *actually felt* by the reader, when they arise, or appear to arise, spontaneously from the poet's feeling, and their effect is not counteracted by the obviousness of cool intention and deliberate artifice" (1 7–8).

Poetry, then, first of all is imitative in that its language is not so much sounds and sounds only, but "sounds significant." Sounding Addisonian, like so many critics of the period, he regards merely descriptive poetry, like landscape painting, as only a part of artistic imitation conveying, as it does, only a clear idea of its object. Poetry is truly imitative "only in proportion as it is capable of raising an ideal *image* or *picture*, more or less resembling the reality of things" (1 12–13). Hence it is the imagination of the artist which creates a language and imagery able to elicit the ways in which nature affects the mind. The passion is described by its sensible effects. Twining puts it succinctly when he says that merely descriptive imitation may offer clear and distinct but also less forceful representation; another kind—he calls it imitative description—offers the image as only the occasion for effecting the principal aim of such description, "the emotion, of whatever kind, that arises from a strong conception of the passion itself. The image carries us on forcibly to the feeling of its internal cause." Summing up this point, Twining offers his view of the truly imitative, of "*this* description of passions and emotions, by their sensible effects" (1 23). As John Draper puts it:

> *The Dissertation on Poetry Considered as an Imitative Art* points out that poetry by its onomatopoeia and by its denotative and connotative faculties, can represent, portray, "imitate," both objective sense-impressions and subjective feelings and passions. This attitude is at once liberal and definite; and the inclusion of feeling as an object of imitation largely relieves μίμησις of the stigma of the photographic, but it gives instead a sentimental tinge, certainly not inherent in Aristotle or in the idea of creating art according to the Universal Truth.[18]

Continuing, Twining discusses a third kind of imitation produced by fiction, that in which a new relationship is set up—a resemblance between the ideas raised and still other ideas, the ideas raised being in some ways copies or resemblances, but, strictly speaking, new combinations of those general ideas in the poet's mind. Whereas in description imitation "is opposed to actual *impression*, external or internal: in fiction, it is opposed to fact." While illusion is the key part of the effect of both, it is a different kind of illusion in each. "Descriptive imitation may be said to produce *illusive perception*; fictive, *illusive belief*" (I 28).

If one follows the Aristotelian ideas closely, says Twining, then only the fourth and final kind of imitation—dramatic or personative poetry—is proper, possessing, as it does, both immediate and obvious resemblance, with speech imitating speech. At the same time he warns against the notion that Aristotle, deeply influenced by the predominance of tragedy in his age and hence understandably stressing the dramatic element, ruled out the descriptive, sonorous, or fictive kinds of imitation. Indeed, the whole tenor of his essay suggests an openness to a broader concept of imitation while stressing the roots of the word in the Plato–Aristotle dialogue in Greek culture. After all, it was early in his essay when he spoke of descriptive imitation as quite properly imitative in its representation of the "emotions, passions, and other internal movements and operations of the mind" (I 22). It was he who, in the spirit of the sensationalistic philosophies of his time, emphasized the imitative quality of operations of the mind upon experience. So also did he stress the imitative power of the fictive with its capacity to capture truth more vividly and to produce "illusive belief."

This wide-ranging end-of-the-century essay captures much of the speculation typical of the age. It is, to be sure, conservative in its clear respect for the tradition going back to Plato and Aristotle and in its desire to develop categories for talking about a proper imitation. Yet it is never exclusive, never closed to the possibilities of Addison's "pleasures of the imagination" or Burke's "sublime" with their emphasis on the centrality of mind in the capturing and presentation of beauty. Twining stresses the gap that has developed in the late-eighteenth century between those critics who understand "in what senses, and from what original ideas, Poetry was *first* called imitation by Plato and Aristotle" and those who, still finding poetry designated as imitative, nevertheless, "instead of carefully investigating the original meaning of the expression, have had recourse, for its explication, to their own ideas, and have, accordingly, extended it to every sense which the widest and most distant analogy would bear" (1 58). He is a reconciler of the claims of the traditional and the new, emphasizing poetry's new claim to capture a wider-ranging view of nature—both the object and the subject responding to it. He is also a defender of the power of poetry to convey truth as seen by the eyes, understood by the head, and felt by the heart.

NOTES

1. *John Keats* (Cambridge: The Belknap Press of Harvard University Press, 1963), p. 239.

2. P. 9. See also one of many helpful observations in Abrams, *The Mirror and the Lamp*, p. 21: "Gradually, however, the stress was shifted more and more to the poet's natural genius, creative imagination, and emotional spontaneity, at the expense of the opposing attributes of judgment, learning, and artful restraints. As a result the audience gradually receded into the background, giving place to the poet himself, and his own mental powers and emotional needs, as the predominant cause and even the end and test of art."

3. Martin Price pays elaborate tribute to Shaftesbury and his defense of art in *To the Palace of Wisdom: Studies in Order and Energy from Dryden to Blake* (Garden City, N.Y.: Doubleday, 1964), p. 98: "Shaftesbury's theory of art seems to have developed out of his use of the analogy of aesthetic and actual experience in the *Characteristics*, and, with the fragments that make up the *Second Characters*, it is the most complete and impressive theory recorded by an English writer of the age." Citations from Shaftesbury are from his *Characteristics of Men, Manners, Opinions, Times*, ed. John M. Robertson, 2 vols. in 1 (Indianapolis & New York: Bobbs-Merrill, 1964). Volume and page numbers are given in parentheses.

4. Ernest Tuveson, in "Shaftesbury and the Age of Sensibility," *Studies in Criticism and Aesthetics, 1660–1800*, edd. Howard Anderson and John S. Shea (Minneapolis: University of Minnesota Press, 1967), p. 85, develops at great length these phrases describing the artist and the

implications of these phrases for a new way of talking about the mimetic dimension of art. In a crucial section he writes: "When Shaftesbury calls the artist the 'second maker under Jove' he subtly changes the meaning of the ancient phrase. The artist is not imitating an ideal reality, but expressing the 'Harmony, Perception, and Concord,' to use Shaftesbury's favorite words, of his own mind. The work of art is valuable in the end, not as a masterpiece of artistic achievement, but as a successful expression of the artist's quality of soul. In literature, it would follow, such terms as 'invention,' 'disposition,' and 'genre,' would have a changed significance, for in the classical tradition they relate to the objective creation according to impersonal norms. One might say, indeed, that each poet is his own subject, which he realizes more or less well in his own genre. In a larger sense, all poets have one subject, and eventually one genre: all insofar as they share it themselves, reflect and set forth the harmony of the universe."

5. See *An Essay on Taste, Together with Observations Concerning the Imitative Nature of Poetry*, ed. Walter J. Hipple, Jr. (Gainesville, Fla.: Scholars' Facsimiles and Reprints, 1963). All references to Gerard are to this edition; page numbers are in parentheses. I am greatly indebted to Hipple's introductory essay.

6. (London: Dilly; Edinburgh, Creech, 1779). All references to Beattie's work are to this edition, with the page numbers in parentheses.

7. See Volume II of *The Works of Richard Hurd, D.D., Lord Bishop of Worcester*, 8 vols. (London: Cadell & Davies, 1811). All references to Hurd are to this edition, with the page numbers in parentheses.

8. See Volume I of *Lectures on Rhetoric and Belles Lettres*, ed. Harold F. Harding, 2 vols. (Carbondale & Edwardsville: Southern Illinois University Press, 1965). Page numbers are in parentheses.

9. (London: Bechet & Dehondt, 1765). Page numbers are in parentheses.

10. 3 vols. (Edinburgh: Kincaid & Bell, 1762). Volume and page numbers are given in parentheses.

11. In *Eighteenth-Century Critical Essays*, ed. Scott Elledge, 2 vols. (Ithaca: Cornell University Press, 1961), II 872–81.

12. *The Works of James Harris, Esq., With an Account of His Life and Character By His Son, The Earl of Malmesbury* (Oxford: Tegg, 1841). Page references are in parentheses.

13. *Lectures on the Sacred Poetry of the Hebrews*, trans. G. Gregory, ed. Calvin E. Stowe (Boston: Croker & Brewster, 1829). Page references are given in parentheses.

14. See especially in *The Mirror and the Lamp*, p. 77: "While Lowth

79

exemplifies a fairly common tendency in the criticism of his day to emphasize the poetic representation of passion, rather than of people or actions, he is notable for conceiving the poem as a mirror which, instead of reflecting nature, reflects the very penetralia of the poet's secret mind."

15. P. 19: "The two styles, in their opposition, represent basic types: on the one hand fully exernalized description, uniform illumination, uninterrupted connection, free expression, all events in the foreground, displaying unmistakable meanings, few elements of historical development and of psychological perspective; on the other hand, certain parts brought into high relief, others left obscure, abruptness, suggestive influence of the unexpressed, "background" quality, multiplicity of meanings and the need for interpretation, universal-historical claims, development of the concept of the historically becoming, and preoccupation with the problematic."

16. Edd. W. P. D. Wightman and J. C. Bryce (Oxford: Clarendon, 1980).

17. 2 vols. (London: Cadell & Davies, 1812).

18. "Aristotelean 'Mimesis' in Eighteenth-Century England," 395–96.

4

Sir Joshua Reynolds:
Freedom and Tradition

It appears to me therefore, that our first thoughts, that is, the effect which any thing produces on our minds on its first appearance, is never to be forgotten; and it demands for that reason, because it is the first, to be laid up with care. If this be not done, the Artist may happen to impose on himself by partial reasoning; by a cold consideration of those animated thoughts which proceed, not perhaps from caprice or rashness, (as he may afterwards conceit,) but from the fullness of his mind, enriched with the copious stores of all the various inventions which he had ever seen, or had ever passed in his mind. These ideas are infused into his design, without any conscious effort; but if he be not on his guard, he may reconsider and correct them, till the whole matter is reduced to a common-place invention.

Discourse XIII

WHILE SIR JOSHUA REYNOLDS has never been seriously neglected by students of English neoclassicism or of the European Enlightenment in general, his stature as a man of letters, especially as an important aesthetician and critic, has received attention only relatively recently. Frederick Hilles' pioneering *The Literary Career of Sir Joshua Reynolds* traces and documents in great detail Reynolds' education, his reading, his association with great literary figures such as Johnson, Burke, Goldsmith, Boswell, and Garrick, and the widespread attention occasioned by the publication of his *Discourses on Art*.[1] Understandably, it does not focus sharply and analytically on particular issues and problems of aesthetic theory. Those who have chosen to study this theory have, interestingly enough, fallen into roughly three categories. Ellis Waterhouse, for example, seems to sum up the attitude of those who see no underlying themes or patterns in the documents. In the introduction to his attractive collection of Reynolds' paintings, he comments that they are "remarkably well written and a pleasure to read today, except by those who hope to discover a philosophical system from them, and those who, like William Blake, regard the whole traditional system as absurd."[2] Walter Hipple, on the other hand, a distinguished historian of eighteenth-century aesthetics and criticism, sees the neoclassic concern with general and particular at the heart of the *Discourses* and notes the influence of Edmund Burke's ideas on the beautiful and sublime.[3] In the same general vein Robert Wark, whose edition of the *Discourses* is definitive, finds a strong neoclassic orientation with certain late–eighteenth-century reverberations. They are, in his words, "one of the most eloquent, as well as one of the last, presentations of the ideas that dominated European art criticism and theory from the mid-fifteenth to the mid-eighteenth century."[4] W. J. Bate, along with critics like Wilson Clough, sees definite anticipations of romanticism, especially in the later *Discourses*, with their emphasis on new ideas and themes. Bate's remarks on Reynolds, in his *From Classic to Romantic*[5] and later in his provocative introduction to the Reynolds section of his *Criticism: The Major Texts*, suggest a decided development in the critic's thinking over a twenty-year period and regard the later discourses in particular as advancing dramatically different emphases. At one point he compares Reynolds to "the romantic critics of his own day and later" in the use of the word "imagination." In his concluding section he contends: "With Reynolds the door stands open to what is best and most durable in the romantic theory of the imagination."[6]

II

The *Discourses on Art*, while fundamentally eighteenth-century documents, are part of that liberal tradition of neoclassic theory extending as far back as Dryden and as far forward as Samuel Johnson. That tradition, keenly aware of the force of older classical models, of the importance of rules and the imitation of models, of the strong moral and didactic responsibility of the artist, is solidly grounded in a theory of beauty as an idea in the mind drawn from the bed-rock of experience. Reynolds, like other critics still lacking a com-pletely adequate critical vocabulary, struggled to communicate the flexibility and richness of the tradition in response to the new ideas—so vividly articulated in the Anglo-Scottish critics—of nature, imitation, imagination, association, emotion, genius, taste, and a host of others.

Johnson seems so much a part of and a culmination of that eighteenth-century tradition of imitation that I have chosen not to include any extended treatment of him in this essay. It may, how-ever, be useful to consider him briefly at this point in order to high-light the ways in which Reynolds, his contemporary, fellow—Club member, and kindred spirit, anticipates future developments rather than echoes old ones.

Johnson does indeed stand as the last great figure in the classical tradition of imitation, firmly grounded in the pioneering efforts of Aristotle and Horace, in neoclassic codifiers like Sidney, Jonson, and Rymer, in the more flexible theory of Dryden and Pope, yet keenly aware of that staggering body of new critical and psychologi-cal theories gathering strength in the Anglo-Scottish critics we have just examined. Wide-ranging and tolerant in his judgment of the ob-jects of artistic imitation, always ready to defend an appeal from criticism to nature, he nevertheless argues for objective experience—life as lived, the persons and events of the arena of real life—as the central criterion for excellence in a great work. It is this experience that art must imitate and capture. "General nature," "the grandeur of generality" are key terms in his praise of the writer who eschews fad and fashion, outlives his age, and offers the nourishment of truth to succeeding ages.[7] "The irregular combinations of fanciful invention," he writes in the *Preface to Shakespeare*, "may delight a-while, by that novelty of which the common satiety of life sends us all in quest; but the pleasures of sudden wonder are soon exhausted, and the mind can only repose on the stability of truth" (pp. 61–62). Shakespeare is the great exemplar of the ideal of imitation, and Johnson, in spite of reservations, praises him mightily for it. His drama "holds up to his readers a faithful mirrour of manners and of life." His characters "are the genuine progeny of common hu-manity, such as the world will always supply, and observation will always find" (p. 62). Gray's *Elegy Written in a Country Church-yard* "abounds with images which find a mirrour in every mind, and with sentiments to which every bosom returns an echo" (III 441). *The Rape of the Lock*, a poem filled with artificial machinery and elaborate imagery, nevertheless appeals to Johnson. "To the praises which have been accumulated on *The Rape of the Lock* by readers of every class," he argues, "from the critick to the waiting-maid, it is difficult to make any addition" (III 232). In the Popean mock-heroic, "new things are made familiar, and familiar things are made new" (III 233).

Given Johnson's central critical premiss, it is relatively easy to understand his impatience with novelty or gimmickry, with merely subjective expression, with whatever distorts the general to call attention to the particular or the transitory. A work of art must be strong rhetorically; language, imagery, and versification must reveal a certain determinacy, must have qualities that serve to enhance and vivify the truth of poetry. A rich, clear, denotative diction; a controlled, functional imagery; an ordered rhythmic pattern of verse; feeling as a helpmate to truth—these are the Johnsonian values. As W. J. Bate puts it,

> The essential function of poetry—taking precedence over everything else—is "to instruct by pleasing": that is, to heighten awareness and deepen or extend the experience of life, through the magical power of language at its greatest. In the process we see the "classical tradition" of criticism, which extends from Aristotle to the later eighteenth century, and which Johnson inherits, becoming more alive and self-corrective.[8]

Perhaps Johnson's most notable objection is to the conceits of Metaphysical poetry, especially that of Abraham Cowley and John Donne, even though he admires the learning and intellectuality of these writers. "[T]hey cannot be said to have imitated any thing; they neither copied nature nor life; neither painted the forms of matter nor represented the operations of intellect" (I 19). They imitated themselves, were in love with their own ingenuity to such an extent that the image became more important than the reality it supposedly represented. "What they wanted however of the sublime," he contends, "they endeavoured to supply by hyperbole;

their amplification had no limits; they left not only reason but fancy behind them, and produced combinations of confused magnificence that not only could not be credited, but could not be imagined" (I 21). Even in Shakespeare's great drama "the equality of words to things is very often neglected, and trivial sentiments and vulgar ideas disappoint the attention, to which they are recommended by sonorous epithets and swelling figures" (pp. 73–74).

Although seeing the greatness of Milton's heroic poetry, in his *Life of Milton* he expressed grave reservations about the pastoral motif of *Lycidas*, its equation of Milton and Edward King with shepherds driving their flocks together, its strange and at times grotesque manner of expression, its harsh diction, its inappropriate rhymes, its jarring versification. In a passage combining a number of his complaints, he writes, "In this poem there is no nature, for there is no truth; there is no art, for there is nothing new. Its form is that of a pastoral, easy, vulgar, and therefore disgusting: whatever images it can supply are long ago exhausted; and its inherent improbability always forces dissatisfaction on the mind" (I 163).

The poems of William Collins "are the productions of a mind not deficient in fire, nor unfurnished with knowledge either of books or life, but somewhat obstructed in its progress by deviation in quest of mistaken beauties" (III 338). Gray's odes "are marked by glittering accumulations of ungraceful ornaments: they strike, rather than please; the images are magnified by affectation; the language is laboured into harshness. The mind of the writer seems to work with unnatural violence. . . . His art and his struggle are too visible, and there is too little appearance of ease and nature" (III 440).

Pope is, of course, Johnson's great hero, eager not just to satisfy but to excel. His great sense of life and delicate care for rhetorical effect "enabled him to condense his sentiments, to multiply his images, and to accumulate all that study might produce, or chance might supply" (III 223). For Johnson, if Pope is not a poet, then who is? Pope epitomizes that Johnsonian ideal of art as an expansive and moving imitation of the persisting truths of human experience.

Johnson, although not advancing the idea of imitation as we have been studying it, is clearly a figure to be reckoned with, clearly an authoritative figure attempting to articulate the great tradition of classical imitation in sensible and flexible ways that would seem pertinent for eighteenth-century critics. One of those critics was Reynolds, a close friend and admirer of Johnson's, a critic respectful of the past and yet interested in new ways of talking about the creation of art and about its effect on an audience.

III

The *Discourses* cover a period of twenty-one years, from the opening address to a select audience of his fellow-academicians on the opening of the Royal Academy on January 2, 1769, through a series of annual lectures to faculty and students on the occasion of distribution of prizes from December 11, 1769 to December 10, 1790. These are years by no means of critical stability, as the previous chapter has revealed, but rather of great ferment and innovation. Addison on the pleasures of the imagination; Burke on the sublime and the beautiful; Shaftesbury and Hutcheson on enthusiasm and taste; Duff and Young on original genius; Beattie, Gerard, and Twining on imitation—these were just a few of the new critical and aesthetic developments that were in the air and would have touched Reynolds. The neoclassic ideals were being examined from a variety of viewpoints.

The underpinning of Reynolds' aesthetic is the familiar Johnsonian premiss of "general nature." Great art, he argues, must, both early and late, transcend the particular and the transitory to seek out general and unchanging truths. In lines that sound remarkably like Johnson's Imlac in *Rasselas*, he says that the artist "must divest himself of all prejudices in favour of his age or country; he must disregard all local and temporary ornaments, and look only on those general habits which are every where and always the same. He addresses his works to the people of every country and every age; he calls upon posterity to be his spectators, and says with Zeuxis, *in aeternitatem pingo*" (No. III, pp. 48–49). Much later, in Discourse VII, echoing Johnson's *Preface to Shakespeare*, he continues the theme: "What has pleased, and continues to please, is likely to please again: hence are derived the rules of art, and on this immoveable foundation they must ever stand" (No. VII, p. 133). As much as the emphasis is on the general, there is, however, little suggestion of the ideal as an abstraction removed from reality. The ideal does not, as Jean Hagstrum suggests, descend from "supersensory archetypes." "For Reynolds, and for his friend Dr. Johnson, general nature is a synthesis of scattered excellencies, the abstraction of general form and species from particular manifestations. Such general forms are in nature; otherwise our search would be in vain. General beauty is like scientific law; it is disclosed not by revelation but by research."[9]

IV

Especially in the first seven discourses, originally published as a unit, Reynolds consistently develops a further theme of discipline and hard work as prerequisites for the expression of the great ideas that are the province of the artist. He assumes—and here the image of his audience looms large—that "an implicit obedience to the *Rules of Art*, as established by the practice of the great MASTERS, should be exacted from the *young* Students" (No. I, p. 17). These rules are not to be seen as shackles; they are regarded as such "only to men of no genius; as that armour, which upon the strong is an ornament and a defence, upon the weak and mis-shapen becomes a load, and cripples the body which it was made to protect" (No. I, p. 17). The rules are best learned by imitating the Masters, the Greeks, Raphael, and Michelangelo, and although Reynolds' attitude toward imitation will change when he moves beyond advising beginners, there is throughout the *Discourses* a wariness about trusting to one's own powers, about original genius, and a strong emphasis on knowing and even entering into a creative rivalry with the Masters. There is a quality of intense urgency about much of his advice to would-be painters, a sense of the arts as a vital part of human life: "From the remains of the works of the antients the modern arts were revived, and it is by their means that they must be restored a second time. However it may modify our vanity, we must be forced to allow them our masters; and we may venture to prophecy, that when they shall cease to be studied, arts will no longer flourish, and we shall again relapse into barbarism" (No. VI, p. 106). No ceremonial praise for the Masters here. The prophecy of an art-less and tradition-less society and its progressive lapse into an uncivilized state has the ring of an Armageddon-like modernity. Know the tradition of culture and let it liberate your own creative impulses or perish, Reynolds seems to be saying.

Having learned the rules for proper imitation of the Masters, the young artist needs to accumulate experience, to develop a fund of subject matter to be shaped and reshaped in his own art.[10] Like Johnson, Reynolds underlines the helplessness of the human mind to create out of its own unaided resources and the need for materials that can be organized and communicated in rhetorically effective ways. In the second stage of the young artist's development, he is amassing "a stock of ideas, to be combined and varied as occasion may require," is becoming attuned—and here the language sounds like an anticipation of the later classicism of a Matthew Arnold—to "all that has been known and done before his own time" (No. II, p. 26). How much like the Arnold of *Preface to Poems* (1853) Reynolds sounds as he minimizes the kind of art that is concerned merely with self-expression or elegance of style! Like Arnold, he looks for "something either in the action, or in the object, in which men are universally concerned, and which powerfully strikes upon the public sympathy" (No. IV, p. 57).

In the third stage of the artist's development, he is in a position to explore the possibilities of true originality. With his apprenticeship behind him, he can move beyond a merely mechanical kind of imitation. He can concern himself with imitating not so much the work as the artist, with turning not so much to books as to the richness of nature itself. Even in the earlier discourses he had probed this idea of imitation with great intensity, arguing that for a painter "frigid contemplation of a few single models, is no less absurd, than it would be in him who wishes to be a Poet, to imagine that by translating a tragedy he can acquire to himself sufficient knowledge of the appearances of nature, the operations of the passions, and the incidents of life" (No. II, p. 29). The artist should capture the spirit of great models, should be more free; at a certain point he "corrects what is erroneous, supplies what is scanty, and adds by his observation what the industry of his own predecessors may have left wanting to perfection" (No. II, p. 27). Later, in much more eloquent terms, Reynolds will appeal to Edward Young's *Conjectures on Original Composition* (1759) in saying that the artist "that imitates the Iliad . . . is not imitating Homer; only the writer who becomes the master of the general principles and spirit that animate the work can be called the true imitator." "The great business of study is, to form a *mind*, adapted and adequate to all times and all occasions; to which all nature is then laid open, and which may be said to possess the key of her inexhaustible riches" (No. XI, pp. 203–204). In the earlier discourses this idea of originality is, of course, always sharply qualified. Genius is never seen as autonomous, as a completely spontaneous activity; for Reynolds, nothing can come of nothing. On the one hand, he looks for excellences in art that go beyond the mere imitation of nature, for a certain power that engages the imagination. On the other, in a stunning appeal to the Ancients, he contends: "The poets, orators, and rhetoricians of antiquity, are continually enforcing this position; that all the arts receive their perfection from an ideal beauty, superior to what is to be found in individual nature" (No. III, p. 42).

Overriding all other arguments of the *Discourses* is a moving concern with the end or final cause of art, and here Reynolds seems squarely in the neoclassic tradition. Art, whether poetry or painting, exists neither for the self-indulgence of the artist nor for the mere entertainment of the audience. It "is not the eye, it is the mind, which the painter of genius desires to address" (No. III, p. 50). The purpose of art is ultimately moral, but never in any narrow didactic sense. Great art must communicate a sense of life as lived, of the direct encounter with reality; must clear the mind of prejudice and open it to the grandeur and breadth of human possibility. In so doing, it enriches the taste of the audience, cultivates the mind, and puts the appetites in perspective. Ultimately, great art holds out an image of beauty that leads to virtuous action. What we have in such argument is a growing defense of literature and its moral force on more imaginative and emotional grounds.

So much for one vital aspect of the *Discourses*, this lively and vital articulation of the key principles of neoclassic aesthetic theory—the moral purpose of the work of art, its eloquent and persuasive use of language to convey a Truth and Beauty enshrined in the mind, but ultimately lodged in and garnered from experience. As suggested already, these principles are treated in depth in the earlier, especially the first seven, discourses although they never lose their urgency, even in the closing words of the last discourse in 1790.

There is, of course, another side to the aesthetics of Reynolds—not so much a romanticism as a more flexible neoclassicism—a side more liberal in its treatment of nature, imitation, and emotion. As early as the third discourse there is an emphasis, in the spirit of Pope's "grace beyond the reach of art," on beauties in poetry and painting which transcend the mere imitation of nature, although he sees the Ancients providing ample precedent. For Reynolds, as for Johnson, there must be an appeal open "from criticism to nature." The inspired artist, compelled by an image of ideal beauty beyond the pretty details of everyday life, captures the great and sublime. He may have the Masters at his back, but he is not so much intimidated by their work as infected by their spirit. Sounding very much like Burke in the treatise on the sublime, Reynolds carefully distinguishes the sublime from what he calls the elegant: "The Sublime impresses the mind at once with one great idea; it is a single blow: the elegant indeed may be produced by repetition; by an accumulation of many minute circumstances" (No. IV, p. 65). At times he seems to turn from a standard mimetic approach as in the famous statement concerning the higher provinces of poetry and painting, those of Shakespeare or of the Roman or Florentine schools of art. "The mind," he argues enthusiastically, "is to be transported, as Shakspeare expresses it, *beyond the ignorant present*, to ages past. Another and a higher order of things is supposed; and to those beings every thing which is introduced into the work must correspond" (No. XIII, pp. 235–36).

This ability to express what is more internal than external, to stir the heart, to capture the sublime is the true mark of genius, a divine power that transcends the routine study and hard work associated with the early training of the artist. It is a power of original invention; Michelangelo's greatest work, for example, while strong in mechanical excellence, "could therefore proceed only from the most poetical and sublime imagination" (No. XV, p. 273). Again, however, the Reynolds search for balance can be observed. He is always quick to qualify any suggestion of the romantic notion of genius creating out of its own untutored resources. Genius is rare, and most mortals must remain in awe of the rules of the Ancients, must not concern themselves with the merely novel. "The greatest natural genius cannot subist on its own stock; he who resolves never to ransack any mind but his own, will be soon reduced, from mere barrenness, to the poorest of all imitations; he will be obliged to imitate himself, and to repeat what he has before often repeated" (No. VI, p. 99).

In many of his later discussions of genius the powers of imagination and emotion become prominent. They are eloquently praised, and there is very little suggestion of these powers as purely ornamental. The ring of much eighteenth-century psychological speculation pervades Reynolds' observations as he strives to reconcile new with old and to find a language for an alliance. He wants the student–artist "to clear his mind from a perplexed variety of rules and their exceptions, by directing his attention to an acquaintance with the passions and affections of the mind, from which all rules arise, and to which they are all referable" (No. VII, p. 162). The true artistic imitation "significantly imitates nature, then, only insofar as its qualities appear to us and have value for us." As Harvey Goldstein puts it, the artist moves from the lower level of objects to the level of the ideal. Reynolds, he says, identifies the highest art with poetry which "applies itself directly to the imagination 'without the intervention of any kind of imitation'."[11]

V

Poetry is more powerful than painting for Reynolds the teacher, and the pleasures of imagination and feeling are key elements. In lines that echo Shaftesbury and anticipate Hazlitt, he praises the power of poetry over all the emotions, and focuses on the dimension of sympathy. He speaks of "one of our most prevalent dispositions, anxiety for the future. Poetry operates by raising our curiosity, engaging the mind by degrees to take an interest in the event, keeping that event suspended, and surprising at last with an unexpected catastrophe" (No. VIII, pp. 145–46). The poetic imagination supplies more than the painter can produce. In lines that clearly remind us of Addison's discussion of the secondary pleasures of the imagination in *The Spectator*, Reynolds asks the student to consider the painter rendering Eve on a canvas with "a determined form, and his own idea of beauty distinctly expressed." He then asks him to consider "the celebrated description of Eve in Milton's Paradise Lost," which "consists in using only general indistinct expressions," with "every reader making out the detail according to his own particular imagination—his own idea of beauty, grace, expression, dignity, or loveliness" (No. VIII, p. 164). Once again, however, there is the marvelous neoclassic balance. Imagination and emotion, even when they are given special liberties, always serve the higher goals of truth and instruction. "Art effects its purpose by their means; an accurate knowledge therefore of those passions and dispositions of the mind is necessary to him who desires to affect them upon sure and solid principles" (No. VIII, no. 162).

Discourse XIII, delivered on December 11, 1786, seems most urgent in its new ideas, in its re-examination of traditional concepts. Taken out of context, many of its pronouncements are indeed romantic-sounding. They need to be seen, like so many mid- and late-century critical statements, as influenced by developments in psychology and aesthetics. At the same time, in spite of the new mood, Reynolds clings to certain fundamental neoclassic principles, flexibly applied but still subsumed under larger didactic and moral concerns. It might be valuable at this point to look closely at this discourse as an intriguing and fruitful example of a late–eighteenth-century critic's loyalty to his intellectual and artistic background, yet his responsiveness to the psychological and aesthetic currents of his time.

What strikes the reader immediately is the boldness of certain statements. There is the warning against *a priori* theories of art, against rigidly mechanical notions of imitation, against undue empirical preoccupation with nature as simply observed reality, against the minimization of the roles of imagination, taste, and emotion. Take, for example, a statement like the following:

All theories which attempt to direct or control the Art, upon any principles falsely called rational, which we form to ourselves upon a supposition of what ought in reason to be the end or means of Art, independent of the known first effect produced by objects on the imagination, must be false and delusive. For though it may appear bold to say it, the imagination is here the residence of truth. If the imagination be affected, the conclusion is fairly drawn; if it be not affected, the reasoning is erroneous, because the end is not obtained; the effect itself being the test, and the only test, of the truth and efficacy of the means [No. XIII, p. 230].

Human beings, then, must feel truth in their hearts and truth in their imaginations, not in their theoretical principles. And artists must bring the workings of the inner life into their work, must proceed, not from what their predecessors have done or from what seems theoretically acceptable, but from a recognition that what takes place within—in the urgency of individual emotion or in the creations of the imagination—is a vital part of human experience.

VI

Reynolds, in his thirteenth Discourse, unquestionably places strong emphasis on imagination and feeling as key concerns of the poem or painting. He assumes, to use his own words, that these arts "address themselves only to two faculties of the mind, its imagination and its sensibility" (No. XIII, p. 230). Interestingly enough, however, these faculties are seen, not as autonomous powers or as rivals of reason, but as strong forces of a capacious mind. Far from simplistically playing off two compartments of the mind, Reynolds sees a unity of our psychological powers, sees degrees of spontaneity and creativity, all of them fulfilling their roles in the larger scheme of things. "There is," he says, "in the commerce of life, as in Art, a sagacity which is far from being contradictory to right reason, and is superior to any occasional exercise of that faculty, which supersedes it; and does not wait for the slow progress of deduction, but goes at once, by what appears a kind of intuition, to the conclusion" (No. XIII, p. 230).

In his enthusiasm to remove painting from "the vulgar idea of imitation" (No. XIII, p. 233), he argues for its "operating by deception" (No. XII, p. 232), contending that it should at times avoid any overt imitation of external nature. There is an almost radical fervor in other lines in which he warns the artist against not being chained to nature as "things." Particular nature, as he describes it, is not the model for the poet or painter; many arts "set out with a professed deviation from it" (No. XIII, p. 234). Once again it is important to notice the larger framework of Reynolds' remarks on this poetic license. He urges artists to "dare everything" (No. XIII, p. 235), but follows with an emphasis on the goal or final end of such daring, asking: "what can be more daring, than accomplishing the purpose and end of art, by a complication of means, none of which have their archetypes in actual nature?" (No. XIII, p. 235).

Perhaps his most venturesome statements concern the creativity of the mind, the notion of the imagination's possessing an idea of perfect beauty. And indeed they are venturesome as long as the reader does not hear in them sounds of Platonism, on the one hand, or of Expressionism, on the other. It is important to keep in mind, in studying these statements, Reynolds' basic premiss, outlined early in this section, that all ideas of perfect beauty, whether in the creative drive of the artist or in the deepest desires of the audience, are founded on experience—internal or external. Speaking sweepingly, he defends the arts by calling their ultimate purpose "to supply the natural imperfection of things, and often to gratify the mind by realising and embodying what never existed but in the imagination" (No. XIII, p. 244). He sounds at times like a Sir Philip Sidney or a John Milton with the suggestion of art as a way of repairing the ruins created in humankind by Original Sin or of recreating the golden world lost in some remote past. And yet there is little of Sidney's or Milton's religious concern with art's power to make men better Christians. Reynolds' is a more humanistic preoccupation, a need to express art's power to complete or widen or enrich human awareness and possibility. There is, he suggests, a unique power in art itself to bring human beings to a fuller realization of the mystery and power of life, a power not subservient to the concerns of religion or philosophy. Art—with its roots in the workings of the creative imagination—ministers to a human hunger for meaning by imitating the great world beyond but also exploring the winding course of the great world within as it confronts that world beyond or attempts to come to a deeper understanding of itself. While he can see the very essence of poetry depending on the "licence it assumes of deviating from actual nature," he follows those words with others that stress the purpose of such license as "to gratify natural propensities by other means, which are found by experience full as capable of affording such gratification" (No. XIII, p. 234).

94

VII

Reynolds is truly a late-neoclassic theorist, someone who, like Johnson, seems to be writing at the end of the classical tradition of aesthetics and criticism. Neither the reactionary nor the flaming liberal, he is the man of common sense, progressive, modern, intellectually alive. Perhaps because he is an artist himself he can more fully appreciate the rhythms of the human heart and the urgings of the creative power. Yet while recognizing these and desiring to understand and incorporate them into any formulation of an aesthetic, he is in the long run classical or neoclassical in his loyalties. For Robert Wark "one doubts whether there was any artist who strove more conscientiously to reconcile the developing attitudes with what he considered best in the tradition he inherited." [12]

Reynolds' *Discourses,* important and influential documents in any study of eighteenth-, especially late–eighteenth-century, aesthetics and criticism, must occupy a key role at this point in our study. On the one hand, they represent a further stage in the development of the theme of subjectivity, of the importance of the creations of the imagination and the cravings of the human heart in any mature theory of art and criticism. Such a development is all the more notable when we see it in a major figure of the Age of Samuel Johnson, a figure we are so quick to associate with the Johnsonian ideal. On the other hand, the *Discourses,* read straight on and in their entirety, never let us forget their critical inheritance, their rich awareness of the goals of Greek and Roman classicism, of Renaissance humanism, of neoclassical formalism. Armed with this latter sense, we will be quick to see Reynolds less as some latter-day romantic and more as the man-of-letters, the teacher of art history and theory *par excellence,* the critic and theorist of art at the end of an age who sees the values of his inheritance and yet who cannot be insensitive to his own developing aesthetic instincts and to the psychological probings of a new kind of criticism. There is much that is old and much that is new in Reynolds; knowing the key themes of the *Discourses* can only help us to understand and to come to terms with an even greater spirit of change in Wordsworth and the critics and theorists of a more romantic age that follows. We turn our attention to that age now.

NOTES

1. (Cambridge: Cambridge University Press, 1936).

2. *Reynolds* (London: Phaedon; New York: Praeger, 1973), p. 36.

3. See, for example, "General and Particular in the *Discourses* of Sir Joshua Reynolds: A Study in Method," *Journal of Aesthetics and Art Criticism*, 11 (1953), 231–47.

4. Sir Joshua Reynolds, *Discourses on Art* (San Marino, Calif.: Huntington Library, 1959), p. xxiii. All references to the *Discourses* are to this edition. Quotations from the text will be followed by parentheses with the number of particular discourses in roman numerals and the pages from Wark's edition in arabic.

5. Pp. 79–92.

6. P. 256.

7. *Johnson on Shakespeare*, ed. Arthur Sherbo, The Yale Edition of the Works of Samuel Johnson, vol. 7 (New Haven & London: Yale University Press, 1968). References to Johnson's Shakespeare criticism are to this edition and to this volume.

References to Johnson's criticism of other poets are to his *Lives of the English Poets*, ed. George Birkbeck Hill, 3 vols. (Oxford: Clarendon, 1905).

8. *Samuel Johnson* (New York & London: Harcourt, Brace, Jovanovich, 1975), p. 403.

9. *The Sister Arts*, pp. 142–43.

10. See Hipple, *The Beautiful, the Sublime, and the Picturesque*, p. 139: "The entire course of study which Reynolds lays out for the student is a course in imitation, first of the object set before him, then of the manner of great workers in the art, then (while imitation of artists is not discontinued) of the abundance of nature itself. This progressive broadening of the object and manner of imitation culminates in the formation of a mind adequate to all times and all occasions."

11. "*Ut Pictura Poesis*: Reynolds on Imitation and Imagination," *Eighteenth-Century Studies*, 1, No. 3 (March 1968), 227.

12. Reynolds, *Discourses on Art*, p. xv.

III

Toward a Romantic Mimesis:
The Manifesto-Makers

5

Wordsworth and the Romantic Manifesto

The principal object, then, proposed in these Poems was to choose incidents and situations from common life, and to relate or describe them, throughout, as far as was possible in a selection of language really used by men, and, at the same time, to throw over them a certain colouring of imagination, whereby ordinary things should be presented to the mind in an unusual aspect; and, further, and above all, to make these incidents and situations interesting by tracing in them, truly though not ostentatiously, the primary laws of our nature: chiefly, as far as regards the manner in which we associate ideas in a state of excitement.

Poetry is the breath and finer spirit of all knowledge; it is the impassioned expression which is in the countenance of all Science. Emphatically may it be said of the Poet, as Shakspeare hath said of man, 'that he looks before and after.' He is the rock of defence for human nature; an upholder and preserver, carrying everywhere with him relationship and love. In spite of difference of soil and climate, of language and manners, of laws and customs: in spite of things silently gone out of mind, and things violently destroyed; the Poet binds together by passion and knowledge the vast empire of human society, as it is spread over the whole earth, and over all time.

Preface to *Lyrical Ballads* (1850)

WHILE IT IS IMPORTANT not to overestimate the position of Wordsworth as a critic and literary theorist, it is nonetheless essential to note the manifesto quality in the several documents written in conjunction with his *Lyrical Ballads* of 1798. He is after all quite traditional—we remember that he was born in 1770, the Age of Johnson—in his emphasis on the truth of his poetry, on its fidelity to nature, on its power to instruct the reader. He is also keenly aware of changing concepts of imagination, association, and taste which are rooted in the British empirical philosophers and expressed in the Anglo-Scottish critics of the eighteenth century. Many of his ideas of a spirit in nature which informs the poet and is expressed in the work of art are also part of the inheritance he received from philosophers like Shaftesbury and Rousseau. Abrams reminds us that Wordsworth "was more thoroughly immersed in certain currents of eighteenth-century thinking than any of his important contemporaries."[1]

Yet we cannot read much of Wordsworth without becoming aware of how much he made these critical concepts his own, modifying and reshaping them to reflect the needs of a young poet unhappy with the themes and language of much eighteenth-century poetry and eager to find values which seem absent in the religious, political, and educational systems of his time. The sterility of contemporary taste, the need for a new kind of poetry to revive and renovate it, a fresh image of the poet as man of feeling and imagination whose imitations are increasingly oriented toward the inner life— these are but a few of the special contributions he makes to contemporary thinking about literature.

Wordsworth's underlying contribution was a radical questioning of the Enlightenment confidence that man's distinctive nature was intellectual and of the consequent rationalistic psychology and aesthetics that grew out of this faith. His greatest confidence was in the emotions and the imagination as distinctive features of the human being and in the power of external nature to nourish and develop these features. Nature—not an abstract paradigm, not Pope's "one clear, unchanged, and universal light," but a presence that pervades the concrete phenomena around us—is a source of strength which inspires feelings of love and benevolence. Contact with nature may "give us more / Than years of toiling reason." Hence man, as he lives close to nature, is essential man, and the poetry that expresses this relationship is the highest art.

Wordsworth's Preface, in its several versions, needs always to be seen in conjunction with his own poetry, although the theoretical framework of the document advances a quite fresh and innovative theory or theories of poetry.[2] It was, he tells us quite straightforwardly, a partial answer to the request of friends who were eager for the success of the poems and convinced that "a systematic defence" of the theory behind them might produce a poetry "well adapted to interest mankind permanently, and not unimportant in the quality, and in the multiplicity of its moral relations" (I 121).

Wordsworth's Preface is such a defense, an argument for the new poetry of the *Lyrical Ballads*. It proceeds from a remarkably perceptive analysis—really a notable piece of sociological commentary —of the state of contemporary taste. The culture of the time, he argues, has blunted the sensibilities of readers, their capacity to imagine freely and to feel strongly, and a literature of artificiality and sensationalism has developed. Wars and rumors of war, the movement of men from the country to the city where the sameness of routine produces a hunger for shocking incident gratified at every turn—these and other phenomena have created widespread lethargy, indeed, a state of "savage torpor." The words of Shakespeare and Milton are driven from the bookshelves and replaced by blood-and-thunder German tragedies, frantic novels, and silly romances. In the face of this situation, the poet feels embarrassed by his weak efforts to counteract the "general evil." Yet he has a "deep impression of certain inherent and indestructible qualities of the human mind, and likewise of certain powers in the great and permanent objects that act upon it, which are equally inherent and indestructible," and a confidence that great poets will more successfully oppose the "general evil" (I 129, 131).

The new poetry has as its principal object

> to choose incidents and situations from common life, and to relate or describe them, throughout, as far as was possible in a selection of language really used by men, and, at the same time, to throw over them a certain colouring of imagination, whereby ordinary things should be presented to the mind in an unusual aspect; and, further, and above all, to make these incidents and situations interesting by tracing in them, truly though not ostentatiously, the primary laws of our nature: chiefly, as far as regards the manner in which we associate ideas in a state of excitement [I 123, 125].

Wordsworth takes two specific approaches to explain what he is doing in his poetry and to point up critical theory responsive to poetic practice. He has been, he explains, more narrowly mimetic in a great many of the poems; as W. J. B. Owen puts it, he, "as far as the notion of selection defines the activity of the poet, conceived it as a purposive and conscious working on the large mass of 'the real language of men,' undertaken with a view to imitating that language."[3] His plan of imitation is direct; he will, in effect, represent men in action, men close to nature and hence more genuine in their emotions and forceful in their expression. He will represent the strong feelings of others. And so we have the characters of the *Lyrical Ballads*: Goody Blake and Harry Gill, Simon Lee, the man and the little girl in "We are Seven"; Martha Ray of "The Thorn"; Betty Foy and Johnny of "The Idiot Boy." And so we have the language of these poems, the language of strong feeling as expressed by real men and women. Wordsworth's proposal is not for photographic realism, but for a fidelity to humble and rustic life complemented by the poet's gift of coloring this life imaginatively, of entering into the hearts and minds of the characters in order to portray them more effectively. We remember the anguish of Betty Foy as she searches for her son Johnny lost while seeking out a doctor for a neighbor desperately ill:[4]

> Now is she high upon the down,
> Alone amid a prospect wide;
> There's neither Johnny nor his Horse
> Among the fern or in the gorse;
> There's neither Doctor nor his Guide.
>
> "Oh saints! what is become of him?
> Perhaps he's climbed into an oak,
> Where he will stay till he is dead;
> Or sadly he has been misled,
> And joined the wandering gipsy-folk.
>
> "Or him that wicked Pony's carried
> To the dark cave, the goblin's hall;
> Or in the castle he's pursuing
> Among the ghosts his own undoing;
> Or playing with the waterfall."

At poor old Susan then she railed,
While to the town she posts away;
"If Susan had not been so ill,
Alas! I should have had him still,
My Johnny, till my dying day."   (lines 217–236)

Or we hear the sea-captain's stark account of Martha Ray—abandoned with child by her lover:

"I did not speak—I saw her face;
Her face!—it was enough for me;
I turned about and heard her cry,
'Oh misery! oh misery!'
And there she sits, until the moon
Through half the clear blue sky will go;

And when the little breezes make
The waters of the pond to shake,
As all the country know,
She shudders, and you hear her cry,
'Oh misery! oh misery!' "   (lines 188–198)

Or there is the exchange in "Expostulation and Reply" between William, the meditative unbusy speaker, and Matthew, the busy, world-oriented questioner. Matthew would question the contemplative lover of nature:

"Why, William, on that cold grey stone,
Thus for the length of half a day,
Why, William, ist you thus alone,
And dream your time away?"   (lines 1–4)

To which William answers:

"The eye—it cannot choose but see;
We cannot bid the ear be still;
Our bodies feel, where'er they be,
Against or with our will.

"Nor less I deem that there are Powers
Which of themselves our minds impress;
That we can feed this mind of ours
In a wise passiveness. . . .   (lines 17–24)

The second approach, represented by many of the additions to the text of 1802, turns decidedly inward, not at the expense of the persons and phenomena of nature, but as a way of heightening the poet's own passionate experience. Hence, the celebrated definition of poetry as "the spontaneous overflow of powerful feelings" produced by a "man who, being possessed of more than usual organic sensibility, had also thought long and deeply." Wordsworth is quick to guard against the idea of poetry as pure self-indulgence or as escapism of any kind. The poet's intense feelings, he contends, are rooted in a reality beyond the self; there is a collaboration of mind and emotion with nature so that what results is a higher truth. Our feelings are modified and shaped by our thoughts, themselves the representatives of past feelings; "and, as by contemplating the relation of these general representatives to each other, we discover what is really important to men, so, by the repetition and continuance of this act, our feelings will be connected with important subjects. . . ." But such communication is not that of the teacher or rhetorician; readers are not instructed as such. Such poetry teaches in a different way, for out of the continuing interaction of thought and feeling come habits of mind, impulses by the following of which "we shall describe objects, and utter sentiments, of such a nature, and in such connection with each other, that the understanding of the Reader must necessarily be in some degree enlightened, and his affections strengthened and purified" (1 127). Hence his specific description of the poet of the inner universe whose creations outdo those of biography and history, the poet of "Tintern Abbey," *The Prelude*, and the "Immortality Ode."

The true poet is a man speaking directly to men, a man of wide-ranging spirit, of strong feelings and active imagination. He is, to be sure, concerned with truth, but with truth as something immediate, something felt in the blood and translated in vivid expression. Using strongly psychological language to probe poetry's concern with the internal universe, Wordsworth eschews any notion that poetry represents a general or abstract truth dependent for its validity on some external institution, standard, or norm. Poetry offers an individual, concrete truth which is its own testimony "carried alive into the heart by passion" (1 139). The poet imitates but does not copy; his work is the image of man in nature and nature in man and of the continuing interaction of the two.

The true poet is self-conscious, is private not public, is turned more inward than outward. Yet he is deeply in touch with all the materials of experience, but not totally dependent upon them for his creations. He is a "man pleased with his own passions and volitions, and who rejoices more than other men in the spirit of life that is in him; delighting to contemplate similar volitions and passions as manifested in the goings-on of the Universe, and habitually impelled to create them where he does not find them." The poet either discovers a hieroglyphic of the inner life in the wondrous processes of nature or, lacking that hieroglyphic, he shapes his own. Whatever route he follows, the overriding need is to capture the urgency of the spirit's demand for expression, for representation. When not expressing his own emotions, he, by an extraordinary degree of imaginative sympathy, is able "to bring his feelings near to those of the persons whose feelings he describes" (1 138), to enter into their identities and represent them with great sensitivity.[5]

Owen is, of course—using a category of Abrams'—quite right to describe the Preface, with the 1802 additions in mind, as presenting "a poetic almost entirely expressive." With humble and rustic life giving way to greater concern with the poet himself and his own speech as objects of representation in Wordsworth's poetry, it is important to develop aesthetic emphases that match the new subjectivity. The poet, says Owen, "expresses his feelings because they are the representative feelings of humanity; and, because his speech is the expression of feeling, its authenticity is assured."[6] Poetry, we might say, to offer a variation on the T. S. Eliot expression, becomes a subjective correlative, but a correlative nevertheless. Even the dramatic poet, attributing his speech to characters outside of himself, identifies his feelings with those of such characters. Yet even with strongly subjective emphasis there is a sense of responsibility to reality, whether internal or external, of the need to capture and represent both the feelings in themselves and as they touch and are touched by the world around us. Imitation has taken on dramatically different shadings, but its classical foundations can still be observed.

With Aristotle still a powerful authority figure for early–nineteenth-century criticism and with several of his themes still in the background, Wordsworth draws on his familiar argument for the superiority of philosophy to biography and history. The preoccupation of these other disciplines with the particular prevents a full view of essential truth, of "the image of things." The poet "writes under one restriction only, namely, the necessity of giving immediate pleasure to a human Being possessed of that information which may be expected from him, not as a lawyer, a physician, a mariner, an astronomer, or a natural philosopher, but as a Man" (I 139). In effect Wordsworth is offering the highest compliment to the poet, a compliment to the poet's miraculous power to touch men at the level of their essential humanity. The poet "considers man and nature as essentially adapted to each other, and the mind of man as naturally the mirror of the fairest and most interesting properties of nature" (I 140). What a new and different use of the art-as-mirror image we have been following in our study! The mind is no merely passive receiver of outside impressions, but rather a power that holds within itself a force and a variety that is within nature. Indeed, the wonderfully suggestive passage from the preface to *The Excursion* speaks of

> such fear and awe
> As fall upon us often when we look
> Into our Minds, into the Mind of Man—
> My haunt, and the main region of my song.   (lines 38–41)

And the voice of the speaker

> proclaims
> How exquisitely the individual Mind
> . . . .
> . . . .   to the external World
> Is fitted . . .

while proclaiming no less confidently how exquisitely also

> The external World is fitted to the Mind;
> And the creation (by no lower name
> Can it be called) which they with blended might
> Accomplish. . . .   (lines 68–71)

What an intriguing collocation of subject and object in the representation process of art! This is the new defense of literature, indeed, of the humanities themselves.

The climax of the Preface is undoubtedly the full definition of poetry that builds on the previous argument. It is a justly famous definition, but one that is too often glibly quoted instead of being thoughtfully examined. Inherent in the definition is the new sense of mimesis, of poetry as imitative not simply of the actions of men, but also of the emotions. Returning to his earlier definition of poetry as "the spontaneous overflow of powerful feelings," he now begins to qualify in such a way that all interpretation of it as a purely expressive aesthetic seems limited. The powerful emotions, he warns, are "recollected in tranquillity," and when the original flow of feeling has been adequately purified and put in perspective, in act however brief, then "the tranquillity gradually disappears, and an emotion, kindred to that which was before the subject of contemplation, is gradually produced, and does itself actually exist in the mind." This is the way successful composition begins, "but the emotion, of whatever kind, and in whatever degree, from various causes, is qualified by various pleasures, so that in describing any passions whatsoever, which are voluntarily described, the mind will, upon the whole, be in a state of enjoyment" (I 149). No purely expressive theorizing here, but rather a quite conscious method of rendering the inner life in a way that will give it breadth and scope. Feeling for Wordsworth is a deeper awareness rather than a mere gush of sentiment, a more powerful access to deeply human truth than the activities of the rationalizing understanding. As Bate contends, feelings are "educated by thought" and in turn become the foundation-stone of thought.[7]

In this whole process imagination is the wondrous faculty, both in the poet and in the reader, the power that goes beyond image-making to combine and synthesize sensations, to see things as they really are—in their totality and their infinite complexity—and to transfer these realizations into active responses. While not at all as technical as Coleridge in his definitions of imagination and of the imaginative rendering of experience, Wordsworth is notable for the enormous power he attributes to the faculty. Some of his most memorable tributes are in the poetry. Early in *The Prelude* he recalls childhood experiences touched by mystery and a religious sense, and he offers praise to the power of mind that gave shape and meaning to nature. On the one hand, he can remember

> That by the regular action of the world
> My soul was unsubdued.   (II 361–362)

while on the other, he says that

>   A plastic power
> Abode with me; a forming hand, . . .
> . . . .
> . . . . at war
> With general tendency, but, for the most,
> Subservient strictly to external things
> With which it communed.   (II 362–363, 365–368)

He never neglects the claims of an insistent reality outside the mind—a reality of sun, birds, breezes, fountains, storms—and yet that reality is enlarged and enriched by the power of mind.

>   An auxiliar light
> Came from my mind, which on the setting sun
> Bestowed new splendour; the melodious birds,
> The fluttering breezes, fountains that run on
> Murmuring so sweetly in themselves, obeyed
> A like dominion, and the midnight storm
> Grew darker in the presence of my eye:
> Hence my obeisance, my devotion hence,
> And hence my transport.[8]   (II 368–376)

Although there are references to the creative and sympathetic powers of the imagination in the Preface—references already considered in this section—it is in the 1815 Preface and in the Essay Supplementary to the Preface of 1815 that more specific definitions and description are found. In a passage of special importance in a study of imitation, he regards imagination as having "no reference to images that are merely a faithful copy, existing in the mind, of absent external objects; but is a word of higher import, denoting operations of the mind upon those objects, and processes of creation or of composition, governed by certain fixed laws" (III 31). Imagination is active as it confronts experience and organizes it to its own liking. Far from a helpmate merely adorning external reality, it creates and operates in accordance with its own laws. The end product is a "new existence" (III 32), not a petty trifle. Unlike fancy which is given to delight the temporal side of our nature, imagination is given "to incite and to support the eternal" (III 37).

Wordsworth is consistently firm in his emphasis on the autonomy of literature, on the truth of its imitation of life, on the moral influence it exerts on readers. A key passage in the Essay Supplementary to the Preface of 1815 is filled with elements of the new aesthetic. Genius, he says, following the eighteenth-century Anglo-Scottish tradition of original genius so aptly expressed by Edward Young in the *Conjectures on Original Composition,* is quite simply doing well "what is worthy to be done, and what was never done before." Such genius, far from parading the novelty of the self and certainly far from expressing elegantly traditional wisdom, creates new forms for articulating the richness of human experience in all its variety, and the result is "the widening the sphere of human sensibility, for the delight, honour, and benefit of human nature." Genius has a twofold gift, either "the introduction of a new element into the intellectual universe: or, if that be not allowed, it is the application of powers to objects on which they had not before been exercised, or the employment of them in such a manner as to produce effects hitherto unknown" (III 82).

William Wordsworth, poet and critic, can be seen as bringing together many of the new ideas of imitation, imagination, taste, emotion, and association that were gathering force in the later-eighteenth century. His poetry—especially the poetry of the inner life—and the several essays that rationalize the poems are pioneering efforts of a major writer in seeing poetry as an intense representation of men in action and, most important, of the rhythms of the human heart as it struggles to express its joy, its sorrow, its triumphs, its tragedies.

NOTES

1. *The Mirror and the Lamp,* p. 103. See also Engell, *Creative Imagination,* p. 265:
"Wordsworth reflects and rephrases thinkers in the latter half of the

eighteenth century, including Hartley, Gerard, Tucker, Reynolds, Reid, Stewart, Alison, as well as writers who, since the 1770s, had been calling for a 'natural language of passion.'

"In one respect Wordsworth was carrying out theories and values prized by many of the associationist critics he read. Not only did his stress on natural and passionate language belong to a critical program under way while Johnson was still alive, but so did his view of the imagination...."

2. References to the critical theory are to *The Prose Works of William Wordsworth*, edd. W. J. B. Owen and Jane Worthington Smyser, 3 vols. (Oxford: Clarendon, 1974). This is an excellent edition for studying the evolution of Wordsworth's critical writings.

3. *Wordsworth as Critic* (Toronto: The University of Toronto Press, 1969), p. 68.

4. Citations of Wordsworth's poetry are from *The Poetical Works of Wordsworth*, ed. Thomas Hutchinson, rev. ed. Ernest de Selincourt (London: Oxford University Press, 1960).

5. See Owen's interesting comment, *Wordsworth as Critic*, p. 83: "With these points in mind, it would seem reasonable to conclude that, in Wordsworth's view, poetry may emerge from an accurate report of another's passionate utterances, and that selection may, therefore, operate upon this raw material as well as upon that which may emerge from the poet's report of his own emotional experience."

6. Ibid., p. 113.

7. *Criticism: The Major Texts*, p. 334.

8. See also the great Snowdon passage of Book 14 where the mountain epitomizes the power of imagination to shape and give meaning to the mysteries of reality:

> When into air had partially dissolved
> That vision, given to spirits of the night
> And three chance human wanderers, in calm thought
> Reflected, it appeared to me the type
> Of a majestic intellect, its acts
> And its possessions, what it has and craves,
> What in itself it is, and would become.
> There I beheld the emblem of a mind
> That feeds upon infinity, that broods
> Over the dark abyss, intent to hear
> Its voices issuing forth to silent light
> In one continuous stream; a mind sustained

By recognitions of transcendent power,
In sense conducting to ideal form,
In soul of more than mortal privilege.
One function, above all, of such a mind
Had Nature shadowed there, by putting forth,
'Mid circumstances awful and sublime,
That mutual domination which she loves
To exert upon the face of outward things,
So moulded, joined, abstracted, so endowed
With interchangeable supremacy,
That men, least sensitive, see, hear, perceive,
And cannot choose but feel.   (lines 63–86)

6

Shelley:
Poetry as the New Religion

The most unfailing herald, companion, and follower of the
awakening of a great people to work a beneficial change in
opinion or institution, is Poetry. At such periods there is an
accumulation of the power of communicating and receiving
intense and impassioned conceptions respecting man and
nature. The persons in whom this power resides, may often
as far as regards many portions of their nature, have little
apparent correspondence with that spirit of good of which
they are the ministers. But even whilst they deny and abjure,
they are yet compelled to serve, the Power which is seated
upon the throne of their own soul. It is impossible to read the
compositions of the most celebrated writers of the present
day without being startled with the electric life which burns
within their words. They measure the circumference and
sound the depths of human nature with a comprehensive and
all-penetrating spirit, and they are themselves perhaps the
most sincerely astonished at its manifestations; for it is less
their spirit than the spirit of the age. Poets are the hierophants of an unapprehended inspiration; the mirrors of the
gigantic shadows which futurity casts upon the present; the
words which express what they understand not; the trumpets
which sing to battle, and feel not what they inspire; the influence which is moved not, but moves. Poets are the unacknowledged legislators of the world.

A Defence of Poetry

I

PERCY BYSSHE SHELLEY strikes the student of romantic theory as
another of the manifesto-makers of the period, a poet–literary the-

Portions of this chapter have been adapted from my article "The Idea of Mimesis in
Shelley's *A Defence of Poetry*," *British Journal of Aesthetics*, 24 (Winter 1984), 59–64.

orist eager to break with traditional ideas of imitation and of art in general and equally eager to assume a role as promulgator of a new creed with the poet as priest and poetry as his gospel. The swift movement of his ideas and the enthusiasm with which he expresses them seem appropriate to this image.

His *A Defence of Poetry* has a special significance for the students of romantic theory or of literary theory in general in that it offers a great artist's recounting of his own creative life.[1] Through this account, written only eighteen months before his death in 1822, one may study not only the poet's encounter with his own creative drives, but also his most fully formed views on the larger issues of the history and philosophy of poetry. For our purposes it is a stimulating and different account of mimesis, an account not as flamboyantly subjective as one might expect of such an exuberant temperament, but keenly sensitive to the experience and reality that transcend the individual feelings of the artist. It is an aesthetic attuned to the long tradition of mimesis under consideration in these pages and yet forceful in its need to see larger and more expansive possibilities in that tradition.

A Defence of Poetry, it will be remembered, was immediately occasioned by Thomas Love Peacock's essay on *The Four Ages of Poetry*, a mock-historical treatment of the rise, decline, and fall of poetry and an attack on its lack of moral value. Sections like the following capture some of the spirit of Peacock's rhetoric:

> A poet in our times is a semi-barbarian in a civilized community. He lives in the days that are past. His ideas, thoughts, feelings, associations, are all with barbarous manners, obsolete customs, and exploded superstitions. The march of his intellect is like that of a crab, backward. The brighter the light diffused around him by the progress of reason, the thicker is the darkness of antiquated barbarism, in which he buries himself like a mole, to throw up the barren hillocks of his Cimmerian labours.[2]

Shelley's reply, however, transcends the level of polemic and proceeds instead to develop a coherent, if somewhat lyrical, argument for the power and moral force of true poetry. Indeed, one notes almost immediately that poetry for Shelley is so wide-ranging as to include all the arts as well as philosophy, science, political theory, whatever contributes to the good and happy life, to the free and generous society. The new defense of poetry proceeds apace. Poetry is decidedly mimetic, although not so exclusively as Abrams would have it in the four categories (mimetic, pragmatic, expressive, objective) he describes in the history of criticism in *The Mirror and the Lamp*. Shelley's basic premiss is the familiar classical tenet, so closely associated with Aristotle in his *Poetics*, that art should imitate reality, not the merely particular but the general and persisting forms that inform the particular. In Shelley's argument, although the poet truly creates, the creation is no merely self-indulgent fancy; it represents those truths that are common to general nature. And yet the Platonic tinge—the yearning for a poetry that captures a transcendent world—is also there. A poet, he contends, "participates in the eternal, the infinite, and the one; as far as relates to his conceptions, time and place and number are not" (p. 112). Again, a "poem is the image of life expressed in its eternal truth" (p. 115). Homer embodied in his epics the ideal perfection of his age. The tragedies of the Athenian dramatist "are as mirrors in which the spectator beholds himself, under a thin disguise of circumstance, stript of all but that ideal perfection and energy which every one feels to be the internal type of all that he loves, admires, and would become" (p. 121).

II

Given such poetic ideals, one asks necessarily: How does poetry express this ideal perfection? Where is it to be found? Can it be imitated representationally? To what extent is it subjective? How do the mind and feelings enter into the process? What are the peculiar intellectual or imaginative or emotional effects on the readers or the viewers of this mimesis? Shelley offers no predictable answers to these questions, no simplistic romantic formulas springing full-blown from the psyche of the creator. If anything, Shelley's responses, if we return to the Abrams categories mentioned above, reveal a strong sense of what Abrams has called the mimetic tradition and an equally strong need to recognize the claims of the expressive. There is something of both Aristotle and Plato in his argument. Art imitates neither the reality outside the mind exclusively nor the inner surgings of the poetic consciousness. There is an interaction, a collaboration, a concert, a process in which the mind confronts external reality and in which external reality must be touched by the shadings of imagination and feeling that are but more primitive and immediate manifestations of a mysterious and supernatural power called inspiration.

Sounding remarkably Aristotelian as he proceeds historically, Shelley regards poetry as "connate with the origin of man" (p. 109). "In the youth of the world," he argues, "men dance and sing and imitate natural objects, observing in these actions, as in all others, a certain rhythm or order" (p. 111). Each genre, however—dance, song, poem—imitates in a different way; Shelley speaks of a certain order or rhythm belonging to each of these classes of mimetic representation. Yet if familiar associations, even those that have brought delight to an early society, become after a long time "signs for portions or classes of thoughts instead of pictures of integral thoughts"; if poets live on capital, on conventional figurative language, art will soon lose its vitality, will soon become obsolete. If associations are never to be shaped or altered from their original patterns; if poets do not, as Coleridge would say, dissolve, diffuse, and dissipate in order to re-create, "language will be dead to all the nobler purposes of human intercourse" (p. 111).

Using the familiar romantic metaphor of the lyre, Shelley again alludes to the more classical emphasis on art as imitation. "Man," he says, "is an instrument over which a series of external and internal impressions are driven, like the alternations of an ever-changing wind over an Aeolian lyre, which move it by their motion to ever-changing melody." At the same time, man is not a purely passive instrument, a receiver of outside forces. His mind is not merely a mirror reflecting the outside world. He receives but also gives, absorbs but also changes, and the source of this activity is "a principle within the human being, and perhaps within all sentient beings, which acts otherwise than in the lyre, and produces not melody, alone, but harmony, by an internal adjustment of the sounds or motions thus excited to the impressions which excite them" (p. 109). Here the mind reveals its creativity, its power to imitate without duplicating, to reshape the materials of experience into new and more lively, although no less true, forms.

This power of mind so central to the Shelleyan notion of mimesis is, of course, imagination. Early in the *Defence* he describes poetry as " 'the expression of the imagination.' " In poetry, as in human life generally, imagination is the dominant power, surpassing in importance meter, language, and every element. Through it poetry achieves its perfection. "Reason is the enumeration of quantities already known; imagination is the perception of the value of those quantities, both separately and as a whole. Reason respects the differences, and imagination the similitudes of things. Reason is to imagination as the instrument to the agent, as the body to the spirit, as the shadow to the substance" (p. 109). Reason, in a word, unlike imagination, views objects with greater objectivity, and is concerned with things apart from our relation to them.

Imagination is creative; it enters into close union with objects, and colors them with its own peculiar light. The key idea stressed by Shelley in contrasting reason and imagination is inspiration. To him the neoclassic emphasis on imitation of models, on planning and expression, was misplaced. Such an emphasis was the result of the limitedness of the poetical faculty itself. Inspiration is the source of all true poetry, and for this reason even the greatest works of art must fall short of their origins:

> Poetry is not like reasoning, a power to be exerted according to the determination of the will. A man cannot say, "I will compose poetry." The greatest poet even cannot say it: for the mind in creation is as a fading coal, which some invisible influence, like an inconstant wind, awakens to transitory brightness: this power arises from within, like the colour of a flower which fades and changes as it is developed, and the conscious portions of our natures are unprophetic either of its approach or its departure [p. 135].

Great poetry is flashingly original, in close if not in complete touch with something divine, something transcendent. Indeed as the poet is engaged and moved by the vision of a better world, it is already slipping away, and his words are a noble but ultimately limited attempt to recapture—to imitate—the power and beauty of the vision.

III

Poetry, then, for Shelley is indeed the imitation of the ideal, of the universal form which underlies or transcends concrete particulars. It is, however, active imitation in which the imagination brings its power to strengthen that ideal, creates pictures that bring it closer to those with eyes to see and ears to hear. At the same time he challenges all narrow notions of the poet as a moral instructor or of art as overtly didactic. Poetry does indeed produce a moral effect, but by widening and nourishing the quality of our experience. To him the strongest evidence of Milton's genius was his neglect of any direct spelling-out of God's superiority over Satan. So also does he account for the moral effect of Homer's work and for its superiority to Lucan, Tasso, and Spenser. "The Divina Commedia and Paradise Lost," he argues strikingly, "have conferred upon modern mythology a systematic form; and when change and time shall have added one more superstition to the mass of those which have arisen and decayed upon the earth, commentators will be learnedly employed in elucidating the religion of ancestral Europe, only not utterly forgotten because it will have been stamped with the eternity of genius" (p. 130).

If then the poet, in his imitation of nature, does not instruct overtly, in what sense does the reader or viewer learn from mimesis? One thinks, in connection with this question, of John Boyd's useful distinction. Boyd, we recall, sees "two fundamentally different views of poetry itself, one of which sees it as an autonomously meaningful structure, and the other, more rhetorically conceived, which views it as an instrument for molding opinion or moving an audience to action."[3] Shelley is clearly in the mimetic tradition even though the classical idea often seems hard to recognize after the probing of the Anglo-Scottish aestheticians of the eighteenth century and of documents like Wordsworth's Preface to the 1800 edition of the *Lyrical Ballads* and the critical writings of Coleridge and Hazlitt. Such probing had offered a new defense of literature, had increasingly seen art as a structure that holds meaning within itself and that need not point to some external support for its ultimate significance. "We want," he says in exploring why we enjoy imitation, "the creative faculty to imagine that which we know; we want the generous impulse to act that which we imagine; we want the poetry of life: our calculations have outrun conception; we have eaten more than we can digest." Meanwhile the poet, in response, "creates new materials for knowledge, and power and pleasure"; poetry "engenders in the mind a desire to reproduce and arrange them according to a certain rhythm and order which may be called the beautiful and the good" (pp. 134–35). We need to see patterns and meanings in the jumble of events in life. We need more than a slice of life. We need figurative embodiments of meaning. Always the true romantic, Shelley argues that things exist for us as we perceive them. The mimetic power of poetry "compels us to feel that which we perceive, and to imagine that which we know. It creates anew the universe, after it has been annihilated in our minds by the recurrence of impressions blunted by reiteration" (p. 137). There are passages like the above in which, speaking of creation and re-creation, Shelley seems not only to be fashioning a fascinating romantic view of mimesis but also to be anticipating so much of what we find in recent critical theory.

IV

Shelley is expansive in his striking development of ideas about the psychological impact of art on its audience. Poetry, he consistently argues, does not communicate information, does not add to our fund of facts, does not attempt to convince us intellectually. It would rather persuade us emotionally by drawing us into the orbit of metaphor and symbol to feel the force of its imitation; poets "draw into a certain propinquity with the beautiful and the true, that partial apprehension of the agencies of the individual world which is called religion" (p. 112). More so than other arts, poetry, with its medium of language, is "a more direct representation of the actions and passions of our internal being, and is susceptible of more various and delicate combinations, than colour, form, or motion, and is more plastic and obedient to the control of that faculty of which it is the creation" (p. 113).

Whereas ethics may extract and propound poetic axioms and advance tenets to civilize men and build a good society, poetry recognizes something essential about human beings. "The great secret of morals is love; or a going out of our own nature, and an identification of ourselves with the beautiful which exists in thought, action, or person, not our own." Men will be virtuous not because they have been instructed in the creed of a religion or a secular humanism. "A man, to be greatly good, must imagine intensely and comprehensively; he must put himself in the place of another and of many others; the pains and pleasures of his species must become his own." Following on these premisses, Shelley proceeds to develop ideas on the imagination's power to carry out these ideals. It is for him the "great instrument of moral good," and poetry "administers to the effect by acting upon the cause." "Poetry enlarges the circumference of the imagination by replenishing it with thoughts of ever new delight, which have the power of attracting and assimilating to their own nature all other thoughts, and which form new intervals and interstices whose void for ever craves fresh food" (p. 118). In a word, poetry makes us more fully human by engaging us totally in what other men have thought and felt. It nourishes a human hunger which the mere observation and experience of the disconnected and often disjointed events of life do not communicate.

Homer never abdicated his supremacy in this realm of art. Rather than offer allegorical models of bravery, loyalty, and dedication, he invented characters of flesh and blood—Achilles, Hector, and Ulysses, for example—whose imaginative force engaged readers totally. So great was the force of this Homeric characterization on readers "until from admiring they imitated, and from imitation they identified themselves with the objects of their admiration" (p. 116). Poetry for Shelley is not ethics, but pleasing contemplation. It is truly a divine power, lifting, as Plato would have it, the veil that covers the hidden beauty of the world. In so doing, it is the ultimate moral vehicle; it "awakens and enlarges the mind itself by rendering it the receptacle of a thousand unapprehended combinations of thought" (p. 117).

To the Platonic charge that much poetry is immoral, Shelley ironically offers a Platonic defense.[4] Further, poetry is a moral force not only for the individual, but for society. It is, he contends, "indisputable that the highest perfection of human society has ever corresponded with the highest dramatic excellence" (p. 122). With his flair for the spectacular, Shelley, again in a Platonic vein, regards poets as the "hierophants of an unapprehended inspiration," as "the unacknowledged legislators of the world" (p. 140).

Shelley's *Defence of Poetry*, then, offers an enthusiastic yet carefully reasoned *apologia* for imaginative literature. Relying strongly on the idea of mimesis, it nevertheless avoids any description of poetry as mere self-expression. Returning to the more classical idea that poetry imitates the ideal and persisting truths of experience, it adds, however, the romantic notion that it imitates them through the vigorous power of the creative imagination, a power quickened by the breath of inspiration. The overall vision is of poetry as a powerful vehicle of moral education.

NOTES

1. All quotations from Shelley are from Volume VII of *The Complete Works of Percy Bysshe Shelley*, edd. Roger Ingpen and Walter E. Peck, 10 vols. (London: Benn; New York: Gordian, 1965).

2. *The Works of Thomas Love Peacock*, ed. Henry Cole, 3 vols. (London: Bentley, 1875), III 335. For a persuasive and stimulating recent treatment of the Peacock essay, see Stephen Prickett, "Peacock's *Four Ages* Recycled," in the *British Journal of Aesthetics*, 22, No. 2 (Spring 1982), 158–66.

3. *Function of Mimesis*, p. xii.

4. See Joseph E. Baker, *Shelley's Platonic Answer to a Platonic Attack on Poetry* (Iowa City: University of Iowa Press, 1965).

7

Hazlitt:
Imitation and the Quest
for a Romantic Objectivity

Poetry then is an imitation of nature, but the imagination
and the passions are a part of man's nature. We shape things
according to our wishes and fancies, without poetry; but
poetry is the most emphatical language that can be found for
those creations of the mind 'which ecstasy is very cunning in.'
Neither a mere description of natural objects, nor a mere
delineation of natural feelings, however distinct or forcible,
constitutes the ultimate end and aim of poetry, without the
heightenings of the imagination. The light of poetry is not
only a direct but also a reflected light, that while it shews us
the object, throws a sparkling radiance on all around it: the
flame of the passions, communicated to the imagination, reveals to us, as with a flash of lightning, the utmost recesses
of thought, and penetrates our whole being. Poetry represents forms chiefly as they suggest other forms; feelings, as
they suggest forms or other feelings. Poetry puts a spirit of
life and motion into the universe. It describes the flowing,
not the fixed. It does not define the limits of sense, or analyze
the distinctions of the understanding, but signifies the excess
of the imagination beyond the actual or ordinary impression
of any object or feeling.

"On Poetry in General"

IT IS ONLY DURING the past thirty years, and largely due to the pioneering essay of W. J. Bate, that William Hazlitt has emerged as a
major figure in English romanticism, an aesthetician and practical
critic whose ideals of gusto, sympathy, and imagination and whose
judgments on Chaucer, Spenser, Shakespeare, Milton, and his own

contemporaries stand as major contributions to an understanding of the spirit of the age.[1] An unpleasant personality at best, an awkward and consistently hostile man, an unregenerate political liberal, a harried and prolific journalist, a person of stormy love affairs and tempestuous marriages, he nevertheless produced a psychologically-oriented criticism that not only is sensitive to the older classical aesthetic but also bespeaks the new concerns of his contemporaries. He is truly a paradoxical figure: on the one hand, self-centered, boisterous, and contemptuous of adversaries; on the other, preoccupied with a kind of passionate art that sets personality in the background and conveys a rich sense of reality. It is fair to say, at this point in the study of English romanticism, that Hazlitt's earlier reputation as a great familiar essayist, the author of "On Reading Old Books," "The Fight," "My First Acquaintance with Poets," and others, must give way to his role as a central figure in the evolution of romantic aesthetics.

Overriding all the special emphases and techniques of Hazlitt's critical practice is what may be described as a new explicit and implicit manifesto for poetry and for the arts in general. The most profound themes of the manifesto—the uniqueness and autonomy of poetry and its power to represent reality in fresh and original ways—have already been seen in contemporaries like Wordsworth and Shelley, but Hazlitt's distinctive formulation of these themes and his new emphases are quite different. Roy Park, who so perceptively traces the struggle of poetry to liberate itself from the intimidations of scientific abstraction and to replace in stature a philosophy and theology whose credibility had been drastically eroded, succinctly describes the special problem confronted by Hazlitt. That problem, he contends, is "whether poetry is poetry, or whether it is finally explicable only within the framework of a more general metaphysic."[2] In short, does poetry have its own *raison d'être*, a unique inspiration, methodology, and effect, or is it the servant of another master?

We have already studied Wordsworth's memorable attempt, in the Preface to the *Lyrical Ballads*, to assert the uniqueness of poetry to express those deeper and more spiritual truths which transcend the world of fact and particularly to which science addresses itself. Poetry, he contended, does not exist to serve the cause of science or philosophy or history. Poetry's object is "truth, not individual and local, but general, and operative; not standing upon external testimony, but carried alive into the heart by passion; truth which is its own testimony, which gives competence and confidence to the tribunal to which it appeals, and receives them from the same tribunal." Poetry, with its own special goals and methodology, is greater than science, for its mode of dealing with truth is to render it immediate and realizable to the human heart; while science, no less concerned with truth, deals with it in more detached and dispassionate ways.

Shelley and Coleridge share the Wordsworthian and the general romantic preoccupation with new questions at the beginning of the nineteenth century: What is poetry in its essence? Is it simply a more pleasant form of expressing the truths of philosophy and theology? Is its metaphorical and symbolic mode merely an adornment of the deeper truth of hard knowledge? There are Coleridge's searching accounts of symbols as "harmonious in themselves and consubstantial with the truths of which they are conductors" or as "characterized by a translucence of the Special in the Individual or of the General in the Especial or of the Universal in the General. Above all by the translucence of the External through and in the Temporal." The symbol-poem for Coleridge "always partakes of the Reality which it renders intelligible; and while it enunciates the whole, abides itself as a living part in that Unity, of which it is the representative." But more about Coleridge later.

Shelley's *Defence of Poetry*, although a more enthusiastic and less carefully reasoned document than those of Wordsworth and Coleridge, is no less unqualified and confident in its defense of poetry as a form of inspired knowledge which must become the source of man's salvation in an increasingly materialistic world.

The new mission of poetry is clearly set at the beginning of the nineteenth century, then, and Hazlitt, although less evangelical in his mode of expression, is no less urgent in his need to talk about the mission and its implications not just for specific writings, but for criticism and for life itself. He seems consistently interested in poetry's basic roots, its connections with life, the peculiar ways in which it imitates life, and the special character of its impact on human personality.

Poetry, indeed art in general, is for Hazlitt intimately related to experience and to human experience in particular. "All art is built upon nature; and the tree of knowledge lifts its branches to the clouds, only as it has struck its roots deep into the earth" (XVIII 77).[3] It is both intensely personal and strongly impersonal, recognizing the claims of the subject and the equally strong claims of the object, as it struggles to imitate the inner and the outer worlds. It is ultimately a vision of life in its wholeness and not simply a vehicle for the artist's ingenuity or self-expression.

Like so many of his contemporaries, Hazlitt begins with the presumption that poetry is no ordinary gift, no simply elegant way of dealing with the everyday. Citing Bacon as his authority, he sees poetry as a unique mode of communication. It is, he says, "strictly the language of the imagination; and the imagination is that faculty which represents objects, not as they are in themselves, but as they are moulded by other thoughts and feelings, into an infinite variety of shapes and combinations of powers" (V 4). Unlike history which "treats, for the most part, of the cumbrous and unwieldy masses of things, the empty cases in which the affairs of the world are packed," poetry is dedicated to the principle that nothing fully human can be foreign to it. It is not simply a kind of writing; "it is 'the stuff of which our life is made' " (V 2). It moves beyond a mere recital of objects and facts, mere delineation of natural feelings; indeed, it becomes true poetry only when the heightening power of imagination charges objects, facts, and feelings with a new and powerful life. Poetry of this kind becomes the most emphatic of all languages, a language that translates symbolically those desires and yearnings of the human spirit which make man essentially what he is, and which make poetry a vital part of life for both artist and audience.

As we have seen so often in the evolution of the concept of imitation, poetry—art in general—performs its noble tasks of educating, of liberalizing, of widening experience not by the more direct methods of rhetoric but by its unique power to capture the wondrous workings of the imagination when engaged by passion and to stir the reader or listener or spectator by involving him in these workings at the same level of imagination and passion. For Hazlitt we know the reality of nature as we feel its processes, and poetry is our strongest vehicle for achieving this sympathy, this involvement.

"Poetry," writes Hazlitt, "is the high-wrought enthusiasm of fancy and feeling. As in describing natural objects, it impregnates sensible impressions with the forms of fancy, so it describes the feelings of pleasure or pain, by blending them with the strongest movements of passion, and the most striking forms of nature." Its imaginative imitation of the life beyond and the life within the mind makes us fuller human beings. And tragic poetry—the highest form of art—communicates the most sublime passion, moves beyond the dangers of morbid preoccupation with suffering by capturing it imaginatively and stirring us to see its larger significance, "and in the rapid whirl of events, lifts us from the depths of woe to the highest contemplations on human life" (v 4–5).

Hazlitt's literary theory can perhaps be best understood in the light of this recurring emphasis on imaginative and emotional strength as the central excellence of a work of art. Before proceeding to any critical consideration of form or technique, he must be satisfied that this criterion is fulfilled. "Poetry is the language of the imagination and the passions," he writes in his essay "On Poetry in General." "It relates to whatever gives immediate pleasure or pain to the human mind. It comes home to the bosoms and businesses of men; for nothing but what so comes home to them in the most general and intelligible shape, can be a subject for poetry." Poetry is the strongest expression we can give to our conception of anything—Hazlitt seems to be less concerned about neoclassic decorum—whether ordinary or dignified, painful or pleasing (v 1). Gusto, Hazlitt's famous synonym for emotional excitement, is "power or passion defining any object" (IV 77), a definition which blends the inner and the outer life. In the coloring of a Titian "whose heads seem to think" and whose "bodies seem to feel"; in Michaelangelo's forms which "everywhere obtrude the sense of power upon the eye" and in his limbs which "convey an idea of muscular strength, of moral grandeur, and even of intellectual dignity"; in the vital "tangible character" of Rembrandt's portraits; in the Greek statues whose "beauty is power"; in Shakespeare and Milton, in Pope's compliments, Dryden's satires, and Gay's *Beggar's Opera*—in all these and in many others, Hazlitt finds that unique power (IV 77–80).

At the same time as Hazlitt singled out emotion as the dominant source of aesthetic pleasure, he was quick to separate it from a mere outpouring of personal feeling, from mere egocentricity or self-expression. From his earliest writings—witness his 1805 "Essay on the Principles of Moral Action"—he had seen man's emotional nature as essential but potentially dangerous. Moderation was the great ideal; strong emotion must be lodged in the larger reality of persons and things beyond the self, must be proportionate to that which evokes it. As in moral action, so also in art; true greatness involves losing the sense of personal identity in something larger and dearer than our own petty concerns. Shakespeare in this connection is Hazlitt's greatest hero, the dramatist ready in an instant to become the person or thing he would represent. In an age of elaborate critical tribute to Shakespeare, no one pays a higher compliment:

> The striking peculiarity of Shakspeare's mind was its generic quality, its power of communication with all other minds—so that it contained a universe of thought and feeling within itself, and had no one peculiar bias, or exclusive excellence more than another. He was just like any other man, but that he was like all other men. He was the least of an egotist that it was possible to be. He was nothing in himself, but he was all that others were, or that they could become [v 47].

True emotional immediacy, then, is a vigorous and absorbing quality, reflecting not simply an inner world of strong feeling but an outer world touched by this strong feeling. Poetry at its best imitates this vital encounter of inner and outer realities and in the process captures a large and generous vision of experience unavailable in the ordinary goings-on of daily life. Hazlitt is quick to call attention to emotional excess among his contemporary writers. In his judgment the only quality which Rousseau possessed to a noteworthy degree was "extreme sensibility, or an acute and even morbid feeling of all that related to his own impressions, to the objects and events of his life. He had the most intense consciousness of his own existence. . . . His craving after excitement was an appetite and a disease" (IV 88–89). Wordsworth and Rousseau are alike, he contends; in Rousseau's rhapsodical outburst on discovering a periwinkle and Wordsworth's exhilaration at finding the linnet's nest with five blue eggs, "Both create an interest out of nothing, or rather out of their own feelings" (IV 92). Imitation must be of the inner and the outer life, but always with some balance so that strong feeling is matched by a great and worthy object in nature. There is indeed, in the midst of Hazlitt's concern with the claims of the subject, a quest for objectivity of a special kind in his criticism.

Shakespeare and Milton, on the contrary, did not "surround the meanest objects with the morbid feelings and devouring egotism of the writers' own minds" (v 53). Their power over readers comes from their deeper sense of what is compelling in the events of life or the workings of the human heart. Shakespeare is everyone and no one at the same time. Revealing so often the impact of Anglo-Scottish theories of sympathy, he speaks of Shakespeare's having "only to think of any thing in order to become that thing, with all the circumstances belonging to it." When he creates a character, real or imaginary, "he not only entered into all its thoughts and feelings, but seemed instantly, and as if by touching a secret spring, to be surrounded with all the same objects, 'subject to the same skyey influences,' the same local, outward, and unforeseen accidents which would occur in reality" (v 48). Hazlitt always stresses the need for the artist's intense understanding of and sympathy with that which is beyond the merely subjective, for a firm grasp of reality that involves mind, imagination, passion. Hence his concept of imitation, although at times echoing the classical, is distinctive. Poetry is "an imitation of nature, but the imagination and the passions are a part of man's nature. We shape things according to our wishes and fancies, without poetry; but poetry is the most emphatical language that can be found for those creations of the mind 'which ecstasy is very cunning in.' " Without the heightening power of the imagination, no representation of object or emotions can be complete. Poetry's light is not only direct, but reflected—the light emanating from within—"that while it shews us the object, throws a sparkling radiance on all around it: the flame of the passions, communicated to the imagination, reveals to us, as with a flash of lightning, the inmost recesses of thought, and penetrates our whole being" (v 3).

More specifically, imitation is the product of genius, an essentially imaginative activity that stirs the faculty to make comparisons, to realize things more vividly. Genius is—again so many of the Anglo-Scottish critics and aestheticians come to mind—nothing less than "originality," "for the most part, *some strong quality in the mind, answering to and bringing out some new and striking quality in nature.*" And it operates not by rule, not by the following of models however great, but by imagination, "the power of carrying on a given feeling into other situations, which must be done best according to the hold which the feeling itself has taken of the mind." Originality is the key—in Shakespeare, in Rembrandt, in all those who possess this unconscious power—and it is "nothing but nature and feeling working in the mind. A man does not affect to be original: he is so, because he cannot help it, and often without knowing it" (VIII 42–43). True imitation shatters our stereotypes, gives the lie to our ideologies, undercuts our prejudices. It unfolds the variety and complexity of what all too often becomes an abstraction of nature rather than nature itself. True imitation alone can capture meanings beyond facts and events, can locate and heighten those crucial impressions triggered in the mind by passion. "When Lear," says Hazlitt in one of his most memorable examples, "calls upon the Heavens to avenge his cause, 'for they are old like him'; there is nothing extravagant or impious in this sublime identification of his age with theirs; for there is no other image which could do justice to the agonising sense of his wrongs and his despair" (V 4). In Caliban's strange manner and language; in the magnificent climax to Prospero's recounting to his daughter Miranda of their abandonment—"Me and thy *crying* self"; in Macduff's deep but silent sadness on hearing Malcolm's generous "What! man, ne'er pull your hat upon your brows!"; in Cleopatra's imagining of Antony's response to their absence—in so many examples from Shakespeare Hazlitt praises the poet's genius for identifying himself with whomever he would represent and for "pass-[ing] from one to another, like the same soul successively animating different bodies. By an art like that of the ventriloquist, he throws his imagination out of himself, and makes every word appear to proceed from the mouth of the person in whose name it is given." In the world of Shakespeare's imagination—more so than in Chaucer and Milton, two of Hazlitt's other heroes—"everything has a life, a place, and being of its own!" (V 50). Imagination gathers a strength from nature that no other source can provide. At one time it can go beyond the self to identify with its object and achieve a wondrous concreteness and a profound sense of the mysterious depths of experience. At another it can stir the associative power of the mind to make connections that bring the subjective dimension to the fore. It truly reconciles the claims of subject and object, and mediates, as Coleridge would have it, between man and nature.

In all the above is, it would seem, still another example of the new defense of poetry, a defense not necessarily of its ability to give fresh expression to enduring truths or to enliven the tenets of philosophy and religion with speaking pictures. Nor is it a defense based on poetry's ability to take us from the daily confrontation with the goings-on of real life to escapist moments of pleasure and delight. Hazlitt has little patience with those who have "a contempt for poetry"; they cannot, he says, have much respect for themselves or for anything else. It is not "a mere frivolous accomplishment" or a "trifling amusement." It is a vital part of human life, a way of grasping reality and charging it with intensity. As Hazlitt would put it, "We must have some outstanding object for the mind, as well as the eye, to dwell on and recur to—something marked and decisive to give a tone and texture to the moral feelings. Not only is the attention thus reused and kept alive; but what is most important as to the principles of action, the desire of good or hatred of evil is powerfully excited (XII 50). Imagination captures this object and heightens it in such a way that our own imaginations are stirred to see it and our feelings are widened and our awareness broadened so that we become fully human.

Hazlitt, then, along with Wordsworth, Coleridge, Shelley, and others, stands as a major romantic theorist. At its best his theory and criticism have a modern ring, especially his discussions of imitation, genius, imagination, sympathy, and the purpose of art. What stand out most sharply are his persistent quest to justify emotional power—or gusto—as the keystone of great art and his plea for an understanding of this power in more objective ways as an escape from maudlin feeling, participation in the living reality of nature, and expression of this participation with intensity and excitement. It is this search for ways of understanding the objective dimensions of true subjectivity, the impersonality of true personality, and of understanding and articulating the logic of passion that makes his criticism such an interesting and valuable balance to the more evangelical approaches of Wordsworth and Shelley.

NOTES

1. See *Criticism: The Major Texts*, pp. 281–92. See also Herschel Baker, *William Hazlitt* (Cambridge: The Belknap Press of Harvard University Press, 1962); W. P. Albrecht, *Hazlitt and the Creative Imagination* (Lawrence: The University of Kansas Press, 1965); Roy Park, *Hazlitt and the Spirit of the Age: Abstraction and Critical Theory* (Oxford: Clarendon, 1971); John Kinnaird, *William Hazlitt: Critic of Power* (New York: Columbia University Press, 1978); John L. Mahoney, *The Logic of Passion: The Literary Criticism of William Hazlitt* (New York: Fordham University Press, 1981).

2. *Hazlitt and the Spirit of the Age*, p. 1.

3. *The Complete Works of William Hazlitt*, ed. P. P. Howe, 21 vols. (London: Dent, 1930–1934).

IV

Formulating a Romantic Aesthetic

8

Coleridge:
Romantic Imitation and the
New Defense of Literature

> In every work of art there is a reconcilement of the external
> with the internal; the conscious is so impressed on the un-
> conscious as to appear in it; as compare mere letters inscribed
> on a tomb with figures themselves constituting the tomb.
> He who combines the two is the man of genius; and for that
> reason he must partake of both. Hence there is in genius it-
> self an unconscious activity; nay, that is the genius in the
> man of genius. And this is the true exposition of the rule
> that the artist must first eloign himself from nature in order
> to return to her with full effect. Why this? Because if he
> were to begin by mere painful copying, he would produce
> masks only, not forms breathing life. He must out of his
> own mind create forms according to the severe laws of the
> intellect, in order to generate in himself that co-ordination
> of freedom and law, that involution of obedience in the
> prescript, and of the prescript in the impulse to obey, which
> assimilates him to nature, and enables him to understand her.
>
> "On Poesy or Art"

I

IN A SENSE Samuel Taylor Coleridge is the spokesman for the whole
movement toward the romantic in English literature and critical
theory. He amplifies and clarifies ideas more generally expressed
in Wordsworth and Shelley; he undoubtedly influenced Hazlitt and
Keats. His was an erratic temperament and personality, promising
much and often delivering less. His was a mind of tremendous po-
tential, not all of which was brought to fulfillment, brilliant at
some times, somewhat obtuse and even obfuscatory at others.[1]

A precocious, imaginative child, the young Coleridge was given to reading, introspection, and solitary reverie. The life of the mind dominated. Witness his own statement about the ways of his childhood: "I regulated all my creeds by my conceptions, not by my *sight*—even at that age."[2] At Cambridge he read voraciously, especially in highly imaginative and complex philosophical works. Like so many of his literary contemporaries, he was given to a youthful burst of radicalism, dissenting from the Church of England, immersing himself in the rationalistic writings of Hartley and Godwin, and developing an ardent enthusiasm for the French Revolution.

It is important to remember, however, that Coleridge's youthful rationalism and materialism were tempered by a pronounced theism and mysticism. The power of mind always loomed large in his speculations, and this strain would be more fully developed by his readings in Kant, Schelling, and other German philosophers.[3] This early tension between subject and object, between mind and empirical reality, between empiricism and idealism is in large part responsible for the great themes of reconciliation and mediation in Coleridge's life and thought, the need to understand and synthesize the conflicting demands of the abstract and concrete, the universal and the particular in life and art. An understanding of this tension can also illuminate his powerful theorizing on imitation, the nature of poetry, and a variety of other topics.

II

Coleridge sought to articulate a philosophy of nature as a process, one which dwelt not in a world of abstractions, but in the concrete reality experienced by human beings. In a sense, as W. J. Bate suggests, he was trying to steer a middle course between the concreteness prized by the British empiricists and the abstract universal prized in the classical and neoclassical traditions.

Given the vision of nature as organic, the question that immediately suggests itself is: How does the mind cope with, deal with, it? How does the artist represent it? How does the critic judge it? Coleridge posits interesting answers, and the beginning point is his distinction between reason and understanding and his discussion of the fundamental inadequacy of each to capture the variety and complexity of nature. Understanding is chiefly concerned with the particular, with the data of the senses. Reason, on the other hand, is concerned with the universal, the general. Each faculty suffers from a fundamental inadequacy in dealing with a nature in which forms and particulars, abstract and concrete, are continuously interacting. Since beauty is "Multëity in Unity," that "in which the *many*, still seen as many, becomes one,"[4] what is needed is a completing power, a power to capture the universal in the particular, the eternal in the temporal. For Coleridge that power is imagination, the chief means by which we know and imitate reality. He writes about this power in a variety of contexts, some theoretical, some practical. There is, of course, the oft-quoted definition distinguishing the primary and secondary imagination and imagination and fancy.[5] Then there is perhaps the more useful definition in *The Statesman's Manual*, a definition which sees the symbol as product of the imagination's encounter with reality, as that "reconciling and mediatory power, which incorporating the Reason in Images of the Sense, and organizing (as it were) the flux of the Senses by the permanence and self-circling energies of the Reason, gives birth to a system of symbols, harmonious in themselves, and consubstantial with the truths, of which they are the *conductors*."[6]

III

Given these premisses, it is safe to say that for Coleridge literature is concerned with producing a vision of life. It is not merely an expression of feeling. It is concerned, not with the form alone or the concrete particular alone, but with the focal point at which each strengthens and completes the other. It is truly a reconciler of man and nature.

Coleridge is specific in his injunctions and observations concerning imitation in art. Emerson Marks speaks of the "fundamentally Aristotelian cast of his mimetic theory."[7] Imitation is for him—his debt to Kant, Schelling, the Schlegels, German idealism in general notwithstanding—the answer to the question posed earlier in these

pages concerning the way in which the artist represents the wondrous variety of nature and its processes. Posing the question to
himself, he says dramatically: "We must imitate nature! yes, but
what in nature,—all and every thing? No, the beautiful in nature.
And what then is the beautiful? What is beauty?" His answer points
up the organic emphasis of his theory. "It is, in the abstract, the
unity of the manifold, the coalescence of the diverse; in the concrete, it is the union of the shapely (*formosum*) with the vital."
More specifically, art must soar beyond servile copying of "mere
nature" or what he calls the *natura naturata*. "Believe me," he says,
"you must master the essence, the *natura naturans*, which presup-
poses a bond between nature in the higher sense and the soul of
man" (Shawcross, pp. 256–57). Imitation for Coleridge—and he
sounds like a nineteenth-century disciple of Aristotle—is the artist's
way of capturing the persisting truths of experience and rendering
them in self-authenticating forms. "The artist," he says, "must
imitate that which is within the thing, that which is active through
form and figure, and discourses to us by symbols—the *Natur-geist*,
or spirit of nature, as we unconsciously imitate those whom we love;
for so only can he hope to produce any work truly natural in the
object and truly human in the effect" (II 259).

Such a concept of imitation accounts for the richest pleasures of
art. The power of resemblance and difference, so often stressed in
eighteenth-century criticism of the idea of imitation, is, of course,
a strong one. Yet there is a deeper pleasure associated with representation involving an interaction of poet and nature which
ultimately results in a reconciliation of man and nature. Art for
Coleridge humanizes nature by incorporating the thoughts and
emotions of man into everything he beholds and contemplates.
Such imitation involves the external world, to be sure, but in its
essence the inner life and its associations play the vital role. In a remarkable passage from his essay "On Poesy or Art," he reveals not
only his obvious debt to the subjectivity of German idealism, but
also to the Anglo-Scottish critics of the eighteenth century.

> Poetry also is purely human; for all its materials are from the
> mind, and all its products are for the mind. But it is the apotheosis
> of the former state, in which by excitement of the associative

power passion itself imitates order, and the order resulting produces a pleasureable passion, and thus it elevates the mind by
making its feelings the object of its reflexion. So likewise, whilst
it recalls the sights and sounds that had accompanied the occasions
of the original passions, poetry impregnates them with an interest
not their own by means of the passions, and yet tempers the passion by the calming power which all distinct images exert on the
human soul. In this way poetry is the preparation for art, inasmuch as it avails itself of the forms of nature to recall, to express,
and to modify the thoughts and feelings of the mind [Shawcross,
p. 254].

What an extraordinary linking of Aristotelian realism with the
developing romantic subjectivism we have been examining. With
a firm commitment to the power and force of the world beyond, he
nevertheless brings into his considerations the equally strong power
and force of the world within as part of the magical process by
which art is created. Poetry brings the passions to bear on reality,
gives the sights and sounds of reality a new vitality, a wider expanse, and yet the passions never overwhelm, never dominate,
never become ends in themselves. The shapes and colors of external
nature become the vehicles for modifying, shaping, embodying, expressing the complex workings of the mind and heart. The whole
internal and external universes are reconciled; art offers the fullest
vision of nature.

IV

Imagination, then, is the magical power in the process of imitation,
the power that mediates the demands of the concrete and the abstract, capturing them at that moment when they meet and fulfill
each other. In so doing, imagination matches the creative power of
nature itself, outstripping the lesser faculty of fancy which can make
pictures, combine images, but which cannot create and shape. In
its secondary function it violates—quite deliberately—the ordinary
associations of experience, indeed disrupts and dissipates them in
order to create a new view of experience, a view that startles the
reader or spectator into realization.

As suggested in the already-quoted *Statesman's Manual* definition, the end product of the imagination's imitation of nature is symbol. Symbol, so often in the popular mind a vague, emotionally charged word that may suggest any figure of speech—simile, allegory, etc.—is carefully considered. To stay with his own words: symbols are "consubstantial with the truths of which they are the conductors"; they are specifically imitators of process—living, dynamic, unfolding—translators of reality which, by their pervasive force, drive truth home to the human person. Allegory is "but a translation of abstract notions into a picture-language which is itself nothing but an abstraction from objects of the senses; the principal being more worthless even than its phantom proxy, both alike unsubstantial, and the former shapeless to boot." Symbol, on the other hand, "is characterized by a translucence of the Special in the Individual or of the General in the Especial or of the Universal in the General. Above all by the translucence of the Eternal through and in the Temporal." With a strong mimetic emphasis Coleridge argues that the symbol, far from being a personal expression, "always partakes of the Reality which it renders intelligible; and while it enunciates the whole, abides itself as a living part in that Unity, of which it is the representative" (White, p. 30). Symbol is rooted in reality, and yet it is a product of the imagination's interaction with reality; the imagination creates a body of meaning like but not identical with reality. J. A. Appleyard describes it aptly as "an imitation; it has the very form of the original but it has its own incommunicable substance which makes every 'atom' of the same 'form' collectively yet a different thing." It is not reality, but is "analogous to reality."[8]

Furthermore, Coleridge argues, these symbols are "harmonious in themselves"; they do not point to referents to give them ultimate value, but have a life of their own, an inner logic and harmony. As such, symbols are embodiments of meaning which should be taken up in their own terms. How fresh a notion for British criticism of the time, albeit a notion very much in the air in Germany in the aesthetics of the Schlegels, Schelling, and Kant! How pronounced a turning away from more pragmatic or utilitarian views of the function of art toward a more thoroughgoing romantic or even modern view!

V

Interestingly enough, these theoretical speculations about literature and art make their way into Coleridge's more specific observations. His most famous definition of poetry has a decidedly romantic thrust, with an emphasis on the organic quality of the poem and a justification of poetry as a worthy rival of science. "A poem," he argues, "is that species of composition, which is opposed to works of science, by proposing for its *immediate* object pleasure, not truth; and from all other species (having *this* object in common with it) it is discriminated by proposing to itself such delight from the *whole*, as is compatible with a distinct gratification from each component *part*" (BL II 13). Blending subjectivity and objectivity, the demands of nature and those of mind, he views the poet as bringing the whole human psychological process into operation—intellect, imagination, emotion. As a person of strong internal powers, the poet blends, fuses, unifies through the vital mediatory power of the imagination, which can match the creativity of nature, can imitate its organic process, its conflicting rhythms, its muchness in oneness. This power "reveals itself in the balance or reconciliation of opposite or discordant qualities: of sameness, with difference; of the general, with the concrete; the idea, with the image; the individual, with the representative . . ." (BL II 16–17). While performing its mystical power of mediation and reconciliation, blending and harmonizing the natural and the artificial, the imagination consistently gives the palm to nature over art, to the matter over the manner, to sympathy with the poetry over admiration for the poet.

Here and elsewhere there is a strongly objective emphasis in Coleridge's subjectivity, stronger perhaps than in Wordsworth, an emphasis on the poet's ultimate responsibility to nature, however strong the importance and urgency of the poet's feelings may be. Not a mere gush of emotion, poetry is a more objective process, an imitation of experience strengthened by the power of feeling and by the imagination's ability to translate the emotional encounter with that experience into strongly symbolic representations. This emphasis, this unique emphasis, the critic must recognize as he proceeds. Offering what amounts to a guide for critics, Coleridge stresses three things about poetry—its universality, its sensuous imagery, its passion—and charges the critic to allude to them as he proceeds with his craft.[9] Coleridge's reflections on the beauty of poetic imitation again reveal the objective, realistic approach. Beauty for him is no mere subjective phenomenon, triggering a kind of glandular response in the reader by virtue of personal association. It, "in *kind* and not in *degree*, is that in which the *many*, still seen as many, becomes one" (Shawcross, p. 232).

Coleridge, with premises like the preceding as background, brings great strength to the new defense of poetry. As we review some of these premises, we find that the defense revolves ultimately around the idea of poetry as a mediator between man and nature, between a thought and thing, as he says, as distinct from the idea of poetry as self-expression, as escape from the hard realities outside the mind. Poetry humanizes nature, he says, infusing "the thoughts and passions of man into every thing which is the object of his contemplation; color, form, motion, and sound, are the elements which it combines, and it stamps them into unity in the mould of a moral idea" (Shawcross, p. 253). The whole external and internal universe is the concern of poetry and its imitative act. With a sharply Aristotelian emphasis, Coleridge adds the new romantic emphasis on the inner life—on imagination and emotion as vital parts of human life.

What, then, is the ultimate result of the poet's imitation of nature? And what is its impact on an audience? Very much in the tradition of those nineteenth-century critics who eschew ideas of art as didactic, he nevertheless argues for the educative power of imitation, and provides a fresh and distinctive view. Poetry's pleasure comes not from the mere presentation of a thing, but rather from re-presentation. Art is not nature, but the imitator of nature, the articulator of her deepest mysteries; it is "the figured language of thought," rivaling and even outdoing nature by its synthesizing power, holding the variety and complexity of nature in a single image. "Hence nature itself would give us the impression of a work of art, if we could see the thought which is present at once in the whole and in every part; and a work of art will be just in proportion as it adequately conveys the thought, and rich in proportion to the variety of parts which it holds in unity" (Shawcross, p. 255).

VI

Without ever becoming mechanical or reductionist, Coleridge's practical criticism is a vivid demonstration of the power of his theoretical principles. What is notable about that criticism is the way in which theory and practice are blended, the way Coleridge can develop a critical premiss and use a play or a character of Shakespeare's, a poem of Wordsworth's, as a natural way of demonstrating it. Similarly, and even more impressive, he can, at the very moment he is discussing a Shakespeare or a Wordsworth, develop a critical principle of great value. His is the kind of mind that is constantly moving from abstract to concrete, from poem or play to the aesthetic principle being illustrated.

For Coleridge Shakespeare is the artist *par excellence*, not just the one who best illustrates his ideals. Shakespeare is not simply a great literary genius, a master creator of character, a writer of plays beyond comparison. He is no less than an instrument of nature, the artist attuned to her inner vibrations, and hence a master imitator. No mere copy, his work is "a true imitation of the essential principles" (Mackail, p. 185). Art for Coleridge cannot, of course, exist apart from nature, and Shakespeare's poetry and plays are splendid examples of this closeness and of the imitative power of the dramatist. His characters are an endless source of admiration for Coleridge; they are like those in life itself, not talked about, but to be inferred by the reader from the richness of the representation.

Coleridge takes sharp issue with so much previous criticism which had seen Shakespeare as a kind of talented barbarian, a genius in spite of himself. Genius cannot be lawless, he argues, and perhaps the narrowness of critical vision prevents an understanding of a sympathy with the form of the plays. Shakespeare was concerned, not with the merely mechanical form, but with the organic, the living form inherent in a nature that is alive and dynamic; that form is "innate; it shapes, as it developes, itself from within, and the fulness of its development is one and the same with the perfection of its outward form" (Mackail, p. 186).

So often, in examining particular plays and characters, Coleridge's enthusiastic reaction can be summed up in exclamations like "They are like nature," or "Shakespeare imitates nature perfectly." There is, of course, an objective tinge to these responses rooted in his sense that Shakespeare exemplifies a mind becoming that on which it meditates, an artist losing his identity in the nature he represents. Shakespeare, he contends, generally gives us expectation instead of surprise so that our response is not the temporary excitement triggered by the sight of a shooting star, but rather the rich pleasure that comes from viewing a sunrise at the determined moment. Shakespeare trusts nature and hence adheres to the great law that opposites tend to attract and moderate each other. "Passion in Shakespeare," Coleridge argues, "generally displays libertinism, but involves morality." Polonius is "the personified memory of wisdom no longer actually possessed" (Mackail, p. 195). Dogberry illustrates the premiss graphically: "no difficulty for one being a fool to imitate a fool; but to be, remain, and speak like a wise man and a great wit, and yet so as to give a vivid representation of a veritable fool,—*hic labor, hoc opus est*" (Mackail, p. 196).

Shakespeare's keen sense of the processes of nature and his faithful rendering of them make him the ultimate moralist. He, of course, as he holds up the mirror, does represent the immoral, but never exaggerates or flatters it. He has "no innocent adulteries, no interesting incests, no virtuous vice:—he never renders that amiable which religion and reason alike teach us to detest . . ." (Mackail, p. 196). He "followed the main march of the human affections," "assured himself that such and such passions and faith were grounded in our common nature, and not in the mere accidents of ignorance and disease" (Mackail, p. 199). No stereotypes of drunken magistrates or saintly poor men; no "benevolent butchers" or "sentimental rat-catchers" (Mackail, p. 197) populate his world. Everything is according to nature. As life goes, so goes his art and the form in which it is embodied.

In his essay "Shakespeare as a Poet generally," Coleridge has great praise for *Venus and Adonis*. Concentrating on several stanzas for careful examination, he then steps back and generalizes, advancing a basic premiss of his Shakespearean criticism and, one might say, of his criticism generally. The success of the great poet, he contends, can be explained by his combination of "deep feeling" and an "exquisite sense of beauty." By his ability to get beyond himself imaginatively, he made a start. And yet something else must be adduced to explain the greatness of his art with its fuller and more powerful imitation. It is "that affectionate love of nature and natural objects, without which no man could have observed so steadily, or painted so truly and passionately, the very minutest beauties of the external world" (Mackail, p. 175). What better example of Coleridge's wide and generous concept of imitation, of art as the representation of a world of action and a world of feeling and imagination, than the praise he expresses for sections of *Venus and Adonis*. They are good illustrations of that poetic power

> of making everything present to the imagination—both the forms, and the passions which modify those forms, either actually, as in the representations of love, or anger, or other human affections: or imaginatively, by the different manner in which inanimate objects, or objects unimpassioned themselves, are caused to be seen by the mind in moments of strong excitement, and according to the kind of the excitement,—whether of jealousy, or rage, or love, in the only appropriate sense of the word, or of the lower impulses of our nature, or finally of the poetic feeling itself. It is, perhaps, chiefly in the power of producing and reproducing the latter that the poet stands distinct [Mackail, p. 179].

VII

Coleridge's criticism of Wordsworth, his close friend and associate, has justly been regarded as a model of its kind. It is for our purposes a splendid example of the aesthetics of Coleridge being translated into a fair and insightful practical criticism. The quality of fairness may seem an unusual one to mention in a study of this kind, but it simply must be mentioned, given the close friendship and collaboration of Wordsworth and Coleridge before 1810 and the cooling of that friendship after Basil Montagu's unfortunate rendition of Wordsworth's justifiable concern for Coleridge's physical condition.

Coleridge traces the background of the *Lyrical Ballads* of 1798, especially the decision of the two poets to include in the volume subjects both natural and supernatural. With great fairness he focuses on Wordworth's decision to choose humble and rustic characters who would speak the language of real life. His interpretation of Wordsworth's purpose is interesting, using as it does the idea of imitation as a starting point. At the heart of Wordsworth's decision, he continues, was "the naturalness, in *fact*, of the things represented" and furthermore "the apparent naturalness of the *representation*, as raised and qualified by an imperceptible infusion of the author's own knowledge and talent, which infusion does, indeed, constitute it an *imitation*, as distinguished from a mere *copy*" (BL II 43). The poems were to be close to nature and truth.

It is the gap between Wordsworthian ideal and execution that triggers Coleridge's critique of the poems of humble and rustic life. He disagrees with the assumption that the essential passions of the human heart are found in peasants and peasant life. Such a life for him is not necessarily noble. And furthermore the most interesting and affecting of such poems—"Michael," "Ruth," "The Mad Mother," for example—are not necessarily rustic, and the thoughts, actions, and expressions of characters in these poems might be found in every state of life, whether country or town.

Coleridge proceeds to search out and advance a principle underlying his strong reservations about the rustic poems and the imitative process that they reveal. In a famous passage he aligns himself squarely with the Aristotelian idea of imitation:

> I adopt with full faith the principle of Aristotle, that poetry as poetry is essentially *ideal*, that it avoids and excludes all *accident*; that its apparent individualities of rank, character, or occupation must be *representative* of a class; and that the *persons* of poetry must be clothed with *generic* attributes, with the *common* attributes of the class; not with such as one gifted individual might *possibly* possess, but such as from his situation it is most probable before-hand, that he *would* possess [BL II 45–46].

Using "The Idiot Boy" as an example, Coleridge complains of its superficial and ultimately unsuccessful strategies. Wordsworth, he says first of all, has not succeeded in casting the idiocy of the boy and the folly of the mother in a larger context of meaning, and consequently the poem emerges as a burlesque. Neither characters nor expressions are successful imitations of nature. A preoccupation with a narrow kind of realism is the villain of the piece; "imitation, as opposed to copying, consists either in the interfusion of the SAME throughout the radically DIFFERENT, or of the different throughout a base radically the same" (BL II 72).

Moving to a consideration of very specific defects in Wordsworth's poems, Coleridge again seems to use the underpinning of imitation. He feels that too often the poetry lacks elevation of style; indeed, it becomes downright prosaic. Again in an Aristotelian vein, he complains of "not seldom a *matter-of-factness* in certain poems," a "laborious minuteness and fidelity in the representation of objects," "the insertion of accidental circumstances, . . . which circumstances might be necessary to establish the probability of a statement in real life, where nothing is taken for granted by the hearer, but appear superfluous in poetry, where the reader is willing to believe for his own sake" (BL II 126). In complaining about the problem of matter-of-factness, Coleridge is, of course, revealing his own distinction between the truth of fact and fiction, the literature of knowledge and power, and pointing up his confidence in art as an imitation of reality that is a unique way of getting at the truth.

Wordsworth's unsuccessful use of the dramatic form in certain poems—at times the poet's voice is too subdued, at others too dominant—and the problem of an intensity of feeling too great for the subject—the portrait of the child in the "Immortality Ode" comes to mind—are other difficulties cited by Coleridge. In a word, Coleridge's complaints about Wordsworth revolve around two issues, both having to do with imitation: Wordsworth in some of his poems operates with too narrow a concept of imitation, favoring a realism in detail and characterization suitable perhaps for journalism but certainly not for poetry; he also tends toward the obtrusive, not trusting adequately in nature's riches, but rather forcing a theory onto the representation of experience.

VIII

In Coleridge's judgment, Wordsworth's excellences far outweigh his defects: he was most often in tune not just with the thoughts and actions of men but with his own feelings; his best poetry is charged with emotion, with his own and with that of others portrayed by a poet capable of entering the feelings of others and of representing them with intensity and beauty; and with these qualities he achieves a range of universality often lacking in some of the more journalistic ballads in which the effect is one of fact rather than of enduring truth.

In the same vein, although not in the same order of merit, Wordsworth is praised for a perfect fidelity to the richness of nature in his images and descriptions, and this power is associated with the poet's long and sympathetic intimacy with the spirit of nature, a rapport with process that, as it were, triggers a strong and true emotional response. And this sympathy is extended to include man as man. "Such he *is*," says Coleridge; "so he *writes*" (BL II 150).

Coleridge sounds the trumpet for the power of imagination in Wordsworth's poetry "in the highest and strictest sense of the word." In his representations of fancy, things are "not always graceful, and sometimes *recondite*"; the "*likeness* is occasionally too strange, and demands too peculiar a point of view, or is such as appears the creature of predetermined research, rather than spontaneous presentation" (BL II 151). Such is not the case when the imagination is at work, a power that makes him of all modern writers closest to Shakespeare and Milton. Using his own words to suggest what imagination does to all that comes under his view, the power does

> "add the gleam
> The light that never was on sea or land,
> The consecration, and the poet's dream" [BL II 151].

In one of the most extraordinarily fertile sections of the critique of Wordsworth's excellences, Coleridge speaks of the poet's difficulty but not obscurity, of his imaginative power to capture the richest nuances of the inner life susceptible not to neat linguistic formulations but only to symbol. Coleridge is again revealing his own special concept of imitation, Aristotelian at root and yet wonderfully expansive in his inclusion of the inner life and its demands in any adequate concept of experience. How appropriate the concept seems to discuss one of the most inward of Wordsworth's poems, the "Immortality Ode," a poem that bemoans the loss of the "celestial light" of childhood and affirms a "strength in what remains behind," in the imaginative power to recollect and renovate those moments of youthful insight with the sober wisdom of age. The

146

poem, says Coleridge, seeks its own audience, fit though few, an audience "accustomed to watch the flux and reflux of their inmost nature, to venture at times into the twilight realms of consciousness, and to feel a deep interest in modes of inmost being." Time and space and their attributes seem inadequate to capture, to represent, to imitate these realms, these modes, and yet they "cannot be conveyed, save in symbols of time and space" (BL II 147). In this extraordinary justification of the inner life and its representation in art, Coleridge is offering a new apologia for the literature of his time, a literature not always direct in its representation of the external world, forthright in its advancing of moral truths, but at times sinuous and struggling in its quest to find form and meaning in the cravings of the passions and the shapings of the imagination. It is not that he breaks with the past, but that he would reckon with the present and the future and provide a philosophy of imitation able to match the strong subjectivity so apparent in literature and art.

In both the Wordsworth criticism and the Shakespeare criticism, as well as in his more general aesthetic, Samuel Taylor Coleridge becomes the spokesman for that wide-ranging body of critical theory and practice that has been characterized as romantic. Responsive to the strongly subjective dimensions of the manifesto-making Wordsworth and Shelley and to the call for greater objectivity of Hazlitt, his criticism and aesthetics gather these strains together and articulate them with elegance and grace. It is his approach which dominates nineteenth-century critical thought and anticipates so much that we associate with the modern.

NOTES

1. See especially Walter Jackson Bate, *Coleridge* (New York: Macmillan, 1968) and *Criticism: The Major Texts*, pp. 357–64; J. A. Appleyard, *Coleridge's Philosophy of Literature: The Development of a Concept of Poetry, 1791–1819* (Cambridge: Harvard University Press, 1965); J. Robert Barth, s.j., *The Symbolic Imagination: Coleridge and the Romantic Tradition* (Princeton: Princeton University Press, 1977); Owen Barfield, *What Coleridge Thought* (Middletown, Conn.: Wes-

leyan University Press, 1971); John Beer, *Coleridge the Visionary* (New York: Collier, 1962).

2. *Collected Letters of Samuel Taylor Coleridge*, ed. Earl Leslie Griggs, 6 vols. (Oxford: Clarendon, 1956), I 354.

3. See Bate's comment in *Coleridge*, p. 145: "No one who has written on literature—or for that matter the arts generally—has more directly and emotionally felt, and philosophically understood, the claims of the subjective (whether of the idealistic or the British-empirical variety) and at the same time retained so firm a grip on the philosophically objective, the specific, or the claims of the technical. The classical and the romantic, the ideal and the concrete process, reason and feeling, symbol and direct statement, form and mimesis—the list could easily be extended—are equally meaningful. And always, within the theater of his mind, the drama of speculation is one that seeks to combine them—to conceive them as they exist in active interplay and assimilation."

4. See Volume II of *Biographia Literaria by S. T. Coleridge, With his Aesthetical Essays*, ed. J. Shawcross, 2 vols. (Oxford: Oxford University Press, 1907), p. 232. All citations from the aesthetical essays are from this edition, cited hereafter as Shawcross.

5. "The IMAGINATION then I consider either as primary, or secondary. The primary IMAGINATION I hold to be the living Power and prime Agent of all human Perception, and as a repetition in the finite mind of the eternal act of creation in the infinite I AM. The secondary I consider as an echo of the former, co-existing with the conscious will, yet still as identical with the primary in the *kind* of its agency, and differing only in *degree*, and in the *mode* of its operation. It dissolves, diffuses, dissipates, in order to re-create; or where this process is rendered impossible, yet still at all events it struggles to idealize and to unify. It is essentially *vital*, even as all objects (*as* objects) are essentially fixed and dead.

"FANCY, on the contrary, has no other counters to play with, but fixities and definites. The Fancy is considered no other than a mode of Memory emancipated from the order of time and space; and blended with, and modified by that empirical phenomenon of the will, which we express by the word CHOICE. But equally with the ordinary memory it must receive all its materials ready made from the law of association." *The Collected Works of Samuel Taylor Coleridge*. VII. *Biographia Literaria, or Biographical Sketches of My Literary Life and Opinions*, edd. James Engell and W. Jackson Bate, 2 vols., Bollingen Series 75 (London: Routledge & Kegan Paul; Princeton: Princeton University Press, 1981), I 304–305. This edition is hereafter referred to as BL.

6. *The Collected Works of Samuel Taylor Coleridge*. VI. *Lay Sermons*, ed. R. J. White, Bollingen Series 75 (London: Routledge & Kegan Paul; Princeton: Princeton University Press, 1972), p. 29. Hereafter cited as White.

7. *Coleridge on the Language of Verse* (Princeton: Princeton University Press, 1981), p. 48.

8. *Coleridge's Philosophy of Literature*, p. 107. See also Abrams' observation in *The Mirror and the Lamp*, p. 55, that "Of all his contemporaries, Coleridge was the most concerned with the problem of how the poetic mind acts to modify or transform the materials of sense without violating truth to nature."

9. See the famous echo of Milton in "Recapitulation and Summary of the Characteristics of Shakespeare's Dramas" in *Coleridge's Literary Criticism*, ed. J. W. Mackail (London: Frowde, 1908), pp. 188–89. Hereafter cited as Mackail. "It is essential to poetry," he says, "that it be simple, and appeal to the elements and primary laws of our nature; that it be sensuous, and by imagery elicit truth at a flash; that it be impassioned, and be able to move our feelings and awaken our affections."

EPILOGUE

THE PRECEDING PAGES represent at best a beginning for a larger study, one that perhaps concerns itself with the ultimate fate of the classical idea of mimesis or imitation. Yet they are, I think, an important and in some ways a crucial beginning, treating as they do the remote origins of the idea in ancient Greece—especially in the writings of Plato and Aristotle—through its slow process of formulation in Augustan Rome, its doctrinization in medieval and Renaissance theory, and its most elegant and conservative restatement in eighteenth-century England. In watching the stages in the evolution of the idea, we have noted a dramatic process of tightening. From the notion of art as the representation of what is essential in reality beyond the mind, of the forms that emerge through the concrete processes of reality, we have seen the emergence of imitation as copy, as following of models, as purveyor of enduring transcendent truths beyond the arena of ordinary experience. We have observed a concurrent movement of the justification of literature from a view that gives it great autonomy as a vision of truth embodied in structures that have value in themselves, to the Roman and later-medieval–Renaissance view of literature as a rhetorical way of giving energy to the eternal truths, as a speaking picture that can drive home to the mind and heart the hard truths of philosophy and religion.

There has been in this essay an even more important focus on a key episode in the history of criticism. We have seen Restoration and eighteenth-century England as a battleground of old and new, an arena in which the tradition and freedom meet and reach an uneasy accommodation, one in which new ideas and a new psychological venturesomeness stand out in interesting ways. We have been skeptical of the image of a monolithic intellectual and aesthetic climate in the period, and especially of the rather popular notion that the original classical idea of imitation all but died out. As early as Dryden, Addison, and Burke, we have noted the slow push toward a view of literary representation as widening to include the inner life, the passions, the imaginings of human beings—slow to be sure, but there is, especially in Addison and Burke, a strong sense of art's responsibility to reckon with the power of mind and feeling to shape reality, to mold it to their own purposes, to find ways of capturing it which challenge the imagination to catch the nuances of experience. Again concurrently is the strong sense that such imitation of reality—imaginative, symbolic, suggestive—holds within it meaning no less real because it is subjective, indeed more so because it is concerned with the whole range of human experience, inner and outer. What we have is a new defense of subjectivity, of the power within to nourish, broaden, educate.

We have been concerned throughout with the persistence of the idea of art as imitation, have not been ready to see its dying out in the eighteenth century to be replaced by the idea of art as expression of feeling. While the idea changes in Addison, Burke, the Anglo-Scottish critics, it changes in the sense that its scope is widened to include the workings of the psyche as well as the actions of human beings, the internal and external universe.

In the so-called romantic critics, the idea of imitation persists—in the manifesto-makers Wordsworth, Shelley, and Hazlitt, in the more philosophical and systematic Coleridge. Here again, and with a debt to eighteenth-century critics and aestheticians as well as German theorists, a fuller and richer idea of imitation develops, and with it a deeper understanding of how art educates by its nurturing and widening of human awareness.

These preceding pages, by viewing episodes in the history of criticism and aesthetics, argue essentially that an idea of imitation persists through the romantics, an idea that art must balance the persisting truths of reality outside the mind with the exploration of the insistent demands of the inner life. While the manifesto-makers seem to tip the balance at times, there is a remarkable effort to recognize and to justify the claims of subject and object, to justify literature as a full representation of the full life.

Where criticism and aesthetics move after Hazlitt and Keats is another story. Perhaps in John Keble, in John Stuart Mill, in the iconoclastic demands for subjectivity in Wilde and Swinburne, in Pater's obsession with the shimmerings of a world within, imitation does give way to something like an almost purely expressive theory of art. Modernism, whether in the arts or in criticism, certainly stretched the possibilities of imitation to the limit and beyond. Post-Structuralism and Deconstructionism, with their rage for textuality, for a certain unconscious intentionality of language apart from an author or an historical period, would seem to have dealt the death blow. And yet of late there has been, even in the most outspoken and radical theory, a new fascination with mimesis, a desire to explore its usefulness as a concept for understanding art without sacrificing new ideals and approaches.

Understanding the dramatic shift in the evolution of mimesis in Restoration and eighteenth-century England enriches our understanding of the possibilities of the term. In this period mimesis may have taken on its widest and richest meaning, perhaps a meaning lodged in those challenging observations in the *Poetics,* and art may have received its highest tribute as an imitation through the imagination of the lives of human beings—not just their actions, but their feelings, their imaginings, their dreams. Such a theory of mimesis ultimately views literature—the arts generally—as a free and independent vehicle for communicating, for widening experience at all levels—heart and head—by drawing readers and spectators into the closest kind of relationship with the fullness of human action.

Coleridge's words on Wordsworth's "Immortality Ode" come to mind again as we close. The poem, we remember, was for Coleridge meant not for everyone, but for those "accustomed to watch the flux and reflux of their inmost nature, to venture at times into the twilight realms of consciousness, and to feel a deep interest in inmost modes of being." How to imitate, to represent, these realms? This was a key question not just for Coleridge in his attempt to deal with Wordsworth's poem, but for so many critics of the time attempting to deal with a new psychic geography. And so was his answer a key one, one that captures the new criticism dealing with a new kind of poetry. Aspects of time and space are, he contends, inadequate to capture the winding ways of human emotion, and yet—for all their indeterminacy—they are all we have to deal with such experience that "cannot be conveyed save in symbols of time and space."

SELECTED BIBLIOGRAPHY

Abrams, M. H. *The Mirror and the Lamp: Romantic Theory and the Critical Tradition.* New York: Oxford University Press, 1968.

Addison, Joseph. *Critical Essays from The Spectator by Joseph Addison, With Four Essays by Richard Steele.* Ed. Donald F. Bond. Oxford: Clarendon, 1970.

Albrecht, W. P. *Hazlitt and the Creative Imagination.* Lawrence: The University of Kansas Press, 1965.

Alison, Archibald. *Essays on the Nature and Principles of Taste.* Rev. ed. Abraham Mills. New York: Harper & Bros., 1854.

Appleyard, J. A. *Coleridge's Philosophy of Literature: The Development of a Concept of Poetry, 1791–1819.* Cambridge: Harvard University Press, 1965.

Aristotle. *The Basic Works of Aristotle.* Ed. Richard McKeon. New York: Random House, 1941.

Atkins, J. W. H. *English Literary Criticism: The Medieval Phase.* London: Methuen, 1952.

———. *English Literary Criticism: The Renascence.* London: Methuen, 1947.

———. *Literary Criticism in Antiquity.* 2 vols. Cambridge: Cambridge University Press, 1934.

Auerbach, Erich. *Mimesis: The Representation of Reality in Western Literature.* Trans. Willard Trask. Garden City, N.Y.: Doubleday, 1957.

Baker, Herschel. *William Hazlitt.* Cambridge: The Belknap Press of Harvard University Press, 1962.

Baker, Joseph E. *Shelley's Platonic Answer to a Platonic Attack on Poetry.* Iowa City: University of Iowa Press, 1965.

Barfield, Owen. *What Coleridge Thought.* Middletown, Conn.: Wesleyan University Press, 1971.

Barth, J. Robert, s.j. *The Symbolic Imagination: Coleridge and the Romantic Tradition.* Princeton: Princeton University Press, 1977.

Bate, Walter Jackson. *Coleridge.* New York: Macmillan, 1968.

———. *From Classic to Romantic: Premises of Taste in Eighteenth-Century England.* New York: Harper & Row, 1961.

――. *John Keats.* Cambridge: The Belknap Press of Harvard University Press, 1963.

――. *Samuel Johnson.* New York: Harcourt, Brace, Jovanovich, 1975.

――. "The Sympathetic Imagination in Eighteenth-Century English Criticism." *ELH*, 12 (1945), 144–64.

Beattie, James. *Essays: On Poetry and Music as They Affect the Mind; On Laughter, and Ludicrous Composition; On the Usefulness of Classical Learning.* London: Dilly; Edinburgh: Creech, 1779.

Beer, John. *Coleridge the Visionary.* New York: Collier, 1962.

Blair, Hugh. *A Critical Dissertation on the Poems of Ossian, the Son of Fingal.* London: Bechet & Dehondt, 1765.

――. *Lectures on Rhetoric and Belles Lettres.* Ed. Harold F. Harding. 2 vols. Carbondale & Edwardsville: Southern Illinois University Press, 1965.

Boyd, John, s.j. *The Function of Mimesis and Its Decline.* Cambridge: Harvard University Press, 1968. Repr. New York: Fordham University Press, 1980.

Bredvold, Louis. *The Intellectual Milieu of John Dryden.* Ann Arbor: University of Michigan Press, 1934.

Burke, Edmund. *A Philosophical Enquiry into the Origin of Our Ideas of the Sublime and Beautiful.* Ed. J. T. Boulton. London: Routledge & Kegan Paul; New York: Columbia University Press, 1958.

Butcher, S. H. *Aristotle's Theory of Poetry and Fine Arts.* Ed. John Gassner. 4th ed. New York: Dover, 1951.

Chapman, Gerald W. *Literary Criticism in England, 1660–1800.* New York: Knopf, 1966.

Clough, Wilson. "Reason and Genius—An Eighteenth-Century Dilemma." *Philological Quarterly*, 23 (1944), 33–54.

Coleridge, Samuel Taylor. *Biographia Literaria by S. T. Coleridge, With His Aesthetical Essays.* Ed. J. Shawcross. Oxford: Oxford University Press, 1907.

――. *Coleridge's Literary Criticism.* Ed. J. W. Mackail. London: Frowde, 1908.

――. *Collected Letters of Samuel Taylor Coleridge.* Ed. Earl Leslie Griggs. 6 Vols. Oxford: Clarendon, 1956.

――. *The Collected Works of Samuel Taylor Coleridge.* 16 vols. Bollingen Series 75. London: Routledge & Kegan Paul; Princeton: Princeton University Press, 1969――.

Cooper, Anthony Ashley, Earl of Shaftesbury. *Characteristics of Men, Manners, Opinions, Times.* Ed. John M. Robertson. 2 vols. in 1. Indianapolis & New York: Bobbs-Merrill, 1964.

Crane, R. S. "English Neoclassical Criticism: An Outline Sketch." In *Critics and Criticism: Ancient and Modern*. Ed. R. S. Crane. Abr. ed. Chicago: The University of Chicago Press, 1952. Pp. 372–88.

——. "On Writing the History of English Criticism, 1650–1800." *University of Toronto Quarterly*, 22 (1953), 376–91.

Critics and Criticism: Ancient and Modern. Ed. R. S. Crane. Abr. ed. Chicago: The University of Chicago Press, 1952.

Criticism: The Major Texts. Ed. W. J. Bate. New York: Harcourt, Brace, 1952. Repr. New York: Harcourt, Brace, Jovanovich, 1970.

Draper, John. "Aristotelian 'Mimesis' in Eighteenth-Century England." *PMLA*, 36 (1926), 372–400.

Dryden, John. *An Essay of Dramatic Poesy and Other Critical Essays*. Ed. John L. Mahoney. Indianapolis, New York, & Kansas City: Bobbs-Merrill, 1965.

——. *Essays of John Dryden*. Ed. W. P. Ker. 2 vols. New York: Russell & Russell, 1961.

Duff, William. *An Essay on Original Genius and Its Various Modes of Exertion in Philosophy and the Fine Arts, Particularly in Poetry*. Ed. John L. Mahoney. Gainesville, Fla.: Scholars' Facsimiles and Reprints, 1964.

Eighteenth-Century Critical Essays. Ed. Scott Elledge. 2 vols. Ithaca: Cornell University Press, 1961.

Eliot, T. S. *John Dryden: The Poet, the Dramatist, the Critic*. New York: Holliday, 1932.

Engell, James. *The Creative Imagination: Enlightenment to Romanticism*. Cambridge: Harvard University Press, 1981.

The English Romantics: Major Poetry and Critical Theory. Ed. John L. Mahoney. Lexington, Mass., & Toronto: Heath, 1978.

Gerard, Alexander. *An Essay on Taste, Together with Observations Concerning the Imitative Nature of Poetry*. Ed. Walter J. Hipple, Jr. Gainesville, Fla.: Scholars' Facsimiles and Reprints, 1963.

Goldberg, M. A. *The Poetics of Romanticism*. Yellow Springs, Ohio: Antioch Press, 1969.

Goldstein, Harvey D. "*Ut Poesis Pictura*: Reynolds on Imitation and Imagination." *Eighteenth-Century Studies*, 1, No. 3 (March 1968), 213–35.

Hagstrum, Jean. *The Sister Arts: The Tradition of Literary Pictorialism and English Poetry from Dryden to Gray*. Chicago: The University of Chicago Press, 1958.

Hardy, J. P. *Samuel Johnson: A Critical Study*. London & Boston: Routledge & Kegan Paul, 1979.

Harris, James. *The Works of James Harris, Esq., With an Account of His Life and Character by His Son, The Earl of Malmesbury.* Oxford: Tegg, 1841.

Hartley, David. *Observations on Man, His Frame, His Duty, and His Expectations.* Ed. Theodore L. Huguelet. Gainesville, Fla.: Scholars' Facsimiles and Reprints, 1969.

Havelock, Eric. *Preface to Plato.* Cambridge: Harvard University Press, 1963.

Hazlitt, William. *The Complete Works of William Hazlitt.* Ed. P. P. Howe. 21 vols. London: Dent, 1930–1934.

Heidler, Joseph Bunn. *The History, From 1700 to 1800, of English Criticism of Prose Fiction.* University of Illinois Studies in Language and Literature 12, No. 2. Urbana: The University of Illinois Press, 1928.

Hilles, Frederick. *The Literary Career of Sir Joshua Reynolds.* Cambridge: Cambridge University Press, 1936.

Hipple, Walter. *The Beautiful, the Sublime, and the Picturesque in Eighteenth-Century British Aesthetic Theory.* Carbondale: The University of Southern Illinois Press, 1957.

——. "General and Particular in the *Discourses* of Sir Joshua Reynolds: A Study in Method." *Journal of Aesthetics and Art Criticism,* 11 (1953), 231–47.

Hobbes, Thomas. *The English Works of Thomas Hobbes of Malmesbury.* Ed. Sir William Molesworth. 11 vols. London: Bohn, 1839–1845.

Honour, Hugh. *Neo-Classicism.* New York: Penguin Books, 1968.

Hume, Robert. *Dryden's Criticism.* Ithaca: Cornell University Press, 1970.

Hurd, Richard. *The Works of Richard Hurd, D.D., Lord Bishop of Worcester.* 8 vols. London: Cadell & Davies, 1811.

Jackson, Wallace. *Immediacy: The Development of a Critical Concept from Addison to Coleridge.* Amsterdam: Rodopi, 1973.

——. *The Probable and the Marvelous: Blake, Wordsworth, and the Eighteenth-Century Critical Tradition.* Athens: University of Georgia Press, 1978.

Jensen, H. James. *A Glossary of John Dryden's Critical Terms.* Minneapolis: University of Minnesota Press, 1969.

Johnson, Samuel. *Lives of the English Poets.* Ed. George Birkbeck Hill. 3 vols. Oxford: Clarendon, 1905.

——. *The Yale Edition of the Works of Samuel Johnson.* 11 vols. New Haven & London: Yale University Press, 1958–1982.

Kallich, Martin. *The Association of Ideas and Critical Theory in Eighteenth-Century England: A History of a Psychological Method in English Criticism.* The Hague & Paris: Mouton, 1970.

Kames, Henry Home, Lord. *Elements of Criticism.* 3 vols. Edinburgh: Kincaid & Bell, 1762.

Kermode, Frank. *The Classic: Literary Images of Permanence and Change.* New York: Viking, 1975.

———. *The Sense of an Ending: Studies in the Theory of Fiction.* New York: Oxford University Press, 1967.

Kinnaird, John. *William Hazlitt: Critic of Power.* New York: Columbia University Press, 1978.

Kroeber, Karl. *Romantic Landscape Vision: Constable and Wordsworth.* Madison: University of Wisconsin Press, 1975.

Lipking, Lawrence. *The Ordering of the Arts in Eighteenth-Century England.* Princeton: Princeton University Press, 1970.

Locke, John. *An Essay Concerning Human Understanding.* Ed. Peter H. Nidditch. Oxford: Clarendon, 1975.

Longinus. *On the Sublime.* Ed. W. Rhys Roberts. Cambridge: Cambridge University Press, 1907.

Lowth, Robert. *Lectures on the Sacred Poetry of the Hebrews.* Trans. G. Gregory. Ed. Calvin E. Stowe. Boston: Croker & Brewster, 1829.

Macaulay, Thomas Babington. "Moore's Life of Lord Byron." In *Critical and Historical Essays Contributed to the Edinburgh Review by Lord Macaulay.* Ed. A. J. Grieve. 2 vols. London: Dent; New York: Dutton, 1907. II 613–42.

MacLean, Kenneth. *John Locke and English Literature of the Eighteenth Century.* New Haven: Yale University Press, 1936. Repr. New York: Russell & Russell, 1962.

Mahoney, John L. *The Enlightenment and English Literature.* Lexington, Mass., & Toronto: Heath, 1980.

———. *The Logic of Passion: The Literary Criticism of William Hazlitt.* New York: Fordham University Press, 1981.

Malec, James. *The Arts Compared: An Aspect of Eighteenth-Century British Aesthetics.* Detroit: Wayne State University Press, 1974.

Marks, Emerson. *Coleridge on the Language of Verse.* Princeton: Princeton University Press, 1981.

———. *The Poetics of Reason: English Neoclassical Criticism.* New York: Random House, 1968.

McKeon, Richard. "Literary Criticism and the Concept of Imitation in Antiquity." In *Critics and Criticism: Ancient and Modern.* Ed.

R. S. Crane. Abr. ed. Chicago: The University of Chicago Press, 1952. Pp. 147–75.

Monk, Samuel. *The Sublime: A Study of Critical Theories in Seventeenth-Century England.* New York: Modern Language Association, 1935.

Montgomery, Robert. *The Reader's Eye: Studies in Didactic Literary Theory from Dante to Tasso.* Berkeley & Los Angeles: The University of California Press, 1979.

Orsini, G. N. Giordano. *Organic Unity in Ancient and Later Poetics: The Philosophical Foundation of Literary Criticism.* Carbondale: Southern Illinois University Press, 1975.

Owen, W. J. B. *Wordsworth as Critic.* Toronto: University of Toronto Press, 1969.

Park, Roy. *Hazlitt and the Spirit of the Age: Abstraction and Critical Theory.* Oxford: Clarendon, 1971.

Peacock, Thomas Love. *The Works of Thomas Love Peacock.* Ed. Henry Cole. 3 vols. London: Bentley, 1875.

Plato. *The Dialogues of Plato.* Trans. B. Jowett. New York: Random House, 1937.

Price, Martin. *To the Palace of Wisdom: Studies in Order and Energy from Dryden to Blake.* Garden City, N.Y.: Doubleday, 1964.

Prickett, Stephen. "Peacock's *Four Ages* Recycled." *British Journal of Aesthetics,* 22, No. 2 (Spring 1982), 158–66.

Reynolds, Sir Joshua. *Discourses on Art.* Ed. Robert Wark. San Marino, Calif.: Huntington Library, 1959.

Richardson, Jonathan. *An Essay on the Theory of Painting.* London: Churchill, 1715.

Robertson, J. G. *Studies in the Genesis of Romantic Theory in the Eighteenth Century.* Cambridge: Cambridge University Press, 1923.

Robinson, Forrest. *The Shape of Things Known: Sidney's Apology in Its Philosophical Tradition.* Cambridge: Harvard University Press, 1972.

Shelley, Percy Bysshe. *The Complete Works of Percy Bysshe Shelley.* Edd. Roger Ingpen and Walter E. Peck, 10 vols. London: Benn; New York: Gordian, 1965.

Sidney, Sir Philip. *An Apology for Poetry, or The Defense of Poesy.* Ed. Geoffrey Shepherd. London: Nelson, 1965.

Smith, Adam. *Essays on Philosophical Subjects.* Edd. W. P. D. Wightman and J. C. Bryce. Oxford: Clarendon, 1980.

Sorban, Goran. *Mimesis and Art: Studies in the Origin and Early De-*

velopment of an Aesthetic Vocabulary. Stockholm: Bonnier, 1966.

Spacks, Patricia Meyer. *Imagining a Self: Autobiography and the Novel in Eighteenth-Century England.* Cambridge: Harvard University Press, 1976.

Spurgeon, Caroline. *Five Hundred Years of Chaucer Criticism and Allusion, 1357–1900.* New York: Cambridge University Press, 1925. Repr. New York: Russell & Russell, 1960.

Studies in Criticism and Aesthetics, 1660–1800. Edd. Howard Anderson and John S. Shea. Minneapolis: University of Minnesota Press, 1967.

Tuveson, Ernest. *The Imagination as a Means of Grace: Locke and the Aesthetics of Romanticism.* Berkeley & Los Angeles: University of California Press, 1960.

———. "Shaftesbury and the Age of Sensibility." In *Studies in Criticism and Aesthetics, 1660–1800.* Edd. Howard Anderson and John S. Shea. Minneapolis: University of Minnesota Press, 1967.

Trawick, Leonard M. *Backgrounds of Romanticism: English Philosophical Prose of the Eighteenth Century.* Bloomington: Indiana University Press, 1925.

———. "Hazlitt, Reynolds, and the Ideal." *Studies in Romanticism,* 4 (1965), 240–47.

Twining, Thomas. *Aristotle's Treatise on Poetry, Translated, With Two Dissertations, on Poetical and Musical Imitation.* 2 vols. London: Cadell & Davies, 1812.

Wasserman, Earl R. *Aspects of the Eighteenth Century.* Baltimore: The Johns Hopkins University Press, 1965.

Waterhouse, Ellis. *Reynolds.* London: Phaedon; New York: Praeger, 1973.

Wimsatt, William K., and Brooks, Cleanth. *Literary Criticism: A Short History.* New York: Knopf, 1959.

Wordsworth, William. *The Poetical Works of Wordsworth.* Ed. Thomas Hutchinson. Rev. ed. Ernest de Selincourt. London: Oxford University Press, 1960.

———. *The Prose Works of William Wordsworth.* Edd. W. J. B. Owen and Jane Worthington Smyser. 3 vols. Oxford: Clarendon, 1974.

Wright, William C. "Hazlitt, Ruskin, and Nineteenth-Century Art Criticism." *Journal of Aesthetics and Art Criticism,* 32 (1973), 509–23.

Young, Edward. *Conjectures on Original Composition.* Ed. Edith J. Morley. Manchester: Manchester University Press, 1918.

Youngren, William. "Addison and the Birth of Eighteenth-Century Aesthetics." *Modern Philology,* 79, No. 3 (February 1982), 267–83.

INDEX

Abrams, M. H., 1, 3, 71, 100, 114
Addison, Joseph: backgrounds, 32–35
  his *Spectator* papers "On the Pleasures of the Imagination," 35
  on the primary and secondary pleasures of imagination, 35–37
  his debt to Locke's *Essay Concerning Human Understanding,* 36–37
  connections between the secondary pleasures of imagination and artistic imagination, 36–37
  on the pleasures of imitation, 37–38
  on the imagination perfecting nature, 38–39
  on the sublime, 40
Appleyard, J. A., 138
Aristotle: his response to Plato, 12
  his concept of mimesis, 12–13
  poetry's imitation of "character" and "emotion," 12–13
  poetry justified in its own terms, 14
Auerbach, Erich, 1, 72

Bate, W. J., 23, 34, 50, 82, 121, 134
Beattie, James: backgrounds, 58
  widening the concept of imitation, 58–61
  advancing a theory of the lyric in his analysis of Anacreon and Thomas Gray, 60–61
Blair, Hugh: backgrounds, 64
  citation of Aristotle and Addison as his sources, 64
  distinguishes "Imitation" and "Description," 64
  defends the primitivism of Macpherson, 64–65
Boulton, James, 42, 44

Boyd, John, 2, 11, 14, 117
Bredvold, Louis, 23
Burke, Edmund: backgrounds, 39
  his new approach to the sublime, 41–42
  his distinction between the sublime and beautiful, 64
Butcher, S. H., 13

Chapman, Gerald, 33, 38–39, 50
Clough, Wilson, 82
Coleridge, Samuel Taylor: on the uniqueness of poetry, 123
  on symbol, 123
  his ideas on nature, reason, understanding, imagination, 134–35
  on imitation, 135–37
  his special emphasis on imagination, 137–38
  on symbol and allegory, 138
  on the educative power of art, 139–40
  his practical criticism of Shakespeare, 141–43; of Wordsworth, 143–46
Crane, R. S., 2

Dennis, John, 40
Draper, John, 2, 76
Dryden, John: backgrounds, 22–23
  on inspiration, 23–24
  on imitation, 24–25
  widening the idea of imitation, 26–27
  his *Essay of Dramatic Poesy,* 26–27
  his concern with artistic latitude in his *Defence of an Essay of Dramatic Poesy,* 29–30
  his conservative spirit in his Preface to the *Fables,* 31–32

Eliot, T. S., 22

Gerard, Alexander: backgrounds, 53–54
on how different arts imitate nature, 54
recasting Aristotle's mimesis in new terms, 54–57
art imitating the inner universe, 55–57
on Homer's imitation in the *Iliad*, 57
Goldberg, M. A., 4
Goldstein, Harvey, 91

Hagstrum, Jean, 2, 16, 87
Harris, James: backgrounds, 69
on the power of art to rival reality, 70
following Addison in widening the process of imitation, 70
on the interrelationship of the arts of imitation, 70
poetry as the greatest mimetic art, 70–71
Havelock, Eric, 11
Hazlitt, William: backgrounds, 121–22
his ideas on the uniqueness of poetry, 122, 124
art's relationship to nature, 124
on tragic poetry, 125
on disinterestedness in art, 126
on Shakespeare and Milton and on the lack of disinterestedness in Wordsworth and Rousseau, 126–27
on poetry imitating the inner life, 127
on poetry as product of genius and imagination, 127
Shakespeare's characters examples of true imitation, 128–29
on the unique educative power of poetry, 129–30
Hilles, Frederick, 81
Hipple, Walter, 2, 81
Hobbes, Thomas, 30, 33–34, 48–49, 50

Howard, Sir Robert, 30
Hume, Robert, 29
Hurd, Richard: backgrounds, 61–62
citing Aristotle on imitation, 62
art imitating the internal and external worlds, 62–63
poetry as superior to philosophy, history, other forms of knowledge, 96

Jackson, Wallace, 3
Johnson, Samuel: connections with Reynolds, 82–83
as culmination of the neoclassical critical tradition, 83
his critical flexibility, 83
his practical criticism, 83–85
Jones, Sir William: backgrounds, 66–67
his challenge to Aristotle, 67
praising the inwardness of poetry, 67
his approach to lyric poetry, 67
his use of the terms "description" and "sympathy," 67
the limitations of language for imitation, 67
on imitation in poetry, painting, music, 68–69
Jonson, Ben, 23

Kallich, Martin, 43
Kames, Henry Home, Lord: backgrounds, 65
a less traditional concept of imitation, 65
only painting and sculpture by their nature imitative, 65
echoes Addison in his ideas of beauty and sublimity, 65
using the word "description" to convey the power of language, 65
possibilities and limits of language, 65–66
a new defense of fiction, art, 66
on the power of art to convey a sense of "ideal presence," 66

Locke, John, 34–35, 36, 50
Longinus, 40–41, 72
Lowth, Robert: backgrounds, 71
  concern with Old Testament, with
  ancient religious poetry, 71
  following Aristotle's idea of imitation, 71
  comparing The Book of Job and
  Oedipus the King, 71–72
  on the sublimity of Hebrew poetry, 72–73
  distinguishes "language of reason"
  and "language of passions," 73

Marks, Emerson, 34–35, 135
Montgomery, Robert, 15
Moyle, Walter, 27

Orsini, G. N. Giordano, 2
Owen, W. J. B., 102, 105

Park, Roy, 122
Peacock, Thomas, 113
Plato: his view of reality, 9–10
  the subversive power of imitation,
  10–12
  limitations of poetry, 11

Reynolds, Sir Joshua: backgrounds,
  81–82
  building on Johnson's premiss of
  "general nature," 86–87
  encouraging discipline, imitation
  of models for young artists, 87–
  88
  need for original genius in the experienced student-artist, 88–89
  great art ultimately moral, 89
  the romantic side of his criticism,
  90
  art imitating the passions, 90–91
  poetry more powerful than painting, 91–92
  "Discourse XIII" notable for romantic ideas of imitation, of
  art's power to widen the sensibility, 92–94
Robinson, Forrest, 17
Rymer, Thomas, 30

Shaftesbury, Anthony Ashley Cooper,
  third Earl of: his view of nature,
  51–52
  how nature is touched by art, 52
  on the artist exploring the inner
  life, 52–53
  art as a form of knowledge, 53
Shelley, Percy Bysshe: backgrounds,
  challenging Peacock, 112–13
  advancing the idea of imitation
  and a new defense of literature,
  113
  following Aristotle's lead on imitation, 114–15
  the Platonic tinge in the *Defence
  of Poetry*, 114
  art imitating the internal and external universes, 115–16
  on imagination and imitation,
  115–16
  challenging narrowly didactic
  views of poetry, 117
  poetry regarded as representing
  the inner life, widening the
  range of experience, 118–19
  offering a Platonic defense of
  Platonic charges against poetry,
  120
  on poetry as a form of knowledge,
  119–20
Sidney, Sir Philip: backgrounds, 15–
  16
  his traditionalism, 16
  Aristotelian elements in his *Apology for Poetry*, 16
  on imitation, 16–17
Smith, Adam: backgrounds, 73–74
  on psychological response to the
  arts, 74
  on imitation, 74–75
Sorban, Goran, 4
Spurgeon, Caroline, 31

Twining, Thomas: backgrounds, 75
  his concern with a growing confusion about the idea of imitation, 75
  poetry as "sounds significant," 116
  distinguishes between "descriptive

imitation" and "imitative description," 76
imitation produced by "fiction," 77
"dramatic" imitation, 77
reconciling old and new ideas of imitation, 77–78

Wark, Robert, 82
Waterhouse, Ellis, 81–82
Wordsworth, William: backgrounds, 99–100
his challenge to neoclassical ideals in his Preface to the *Lyrical Ballads*, 100–101
his defense of a new kind of poetry, 101–103

portrait of the new, self-conscious poet, 104–105
the expressive dimension of poetry, 105
a new kind of imitation, 106–107
poetry superior to biography, history, 106
his definition of poetry, 107
new views of the imagination in the 1815 Preface and the Essay Supplementary to the 1815 Preface, 108–109

Young, Edward, 43, 88–89, 109
Youngren, William, 35